*Samuel L. Clemens (Mark Twain) and Major Pond, Mrs. Clemens, Clara Clemens, and Mrs. Pond aboard the S. S. **Warimoo**. August 23, 1895.*

Overland with Mark Twain:
James B. Pond's Photographs and Journal
of the North American Lecture Tour of 1895

Edited by Alan Gribben and Nick Karanovich
with the Assistance of
Mark Woodhouse, Rosemarie Holleran, Jan Kather, and Gretchen Sharlow

A Quarry Farm Volume
Darryl Baskin, General Editor

Center for Mark Twain Studies at Quarry Farm
Elmira College
Elmira, New York
1992

*The editors wish to acknowledge the valuable assistance of Irene Wong
in transcribing and proofreading James B. Pond's journal.*

Copyright © 1992 by The Elmira College Center for Mark Twain Studies at Quarry Farm, Elmira College, Elmira, New York 14901.
Telephone (607) 732-0993. All rights reserved. Published with funding assistance from the Mark Twain Foundation of New York City
and the Wurtele Foundation of Elmira, New York.

ISBN 1-880817-00-4

Table of Contents

Preface
by Nick Karanovich

In May of 1984, book dealer George Robert Minkoff, of Great Barrington, Massachusetts, called me about some photographs and negatives of Mark Twain and a manuscript by Major James B. Pond describing a trip that Pond and Twain took together. George stated that he had seen these materials at another book dealer's shop and would try to secure them and send them to me on approval. In a few days everything arrived.

I read the manuscript and found it to be similar to the one that Pond had published in *Eccentricities of Genius* in 1900 and in a shorter version in the *Saturday Evening Post* of September 29, 1900. The manuscript described the July–August 1895 trip from Mark Twain's summer work place, Quarry Farm at Elmira, New York, to Victoria, Canada, taken by Mark Twain, his wife Olivia, and his daughter Clara, with Pond and his wife Martha. After carefully examining the manuscript I found some sentences and paragraphs alluding to Mark Twain's irascibility, which had been deleted in the versions published in 1900.

In addition, there were approximately twenty pages out of the ninety-three pages of typed and holograph manuscript that were previously unpublished. The unpublished material contained a half-page description of the journey on July 25, along with a one page description of July 28. A three–and–one-half–page portion referred to "Mark Twain's Cigar Case Made of 'The Skin of a Young Lady.'"

Additional descriptions told of the August 11 and August 18 portions of the trip. New were three and one-half pages about the August 1895 *San Francisco Examiner* statement by Mark Twain. Four unpublished pages contained discussions of Pond's revisit to Quarry Farm in September of 1895, along with seven and one-half pages on the "Continuation of Mark Twain's Speech at the Theatre When Puddin Head Wilson Was First Produced." The new material in the manuscript seemed significant. I was thrilled!

Fifty-six photographic prints of the trip accompanied the manuscript. I discovered that about forty of those prints had not been published previously. All of these "drug store" prints appeared to have been made in the 1940s or 50s. Each of the prints had a description written on the reverse side.

Negatives were included from which the fifty-six prints were made. There were one hundred twenty-five of these negatives showing the 1895 journey. The negatives looked—to my untrained eye—original. A quick survey suggested that over one hundred of these negatives had never been published. My mind was racing at fifty miles an hour and my heart was beating even faster. This group of materials was among the finest that could be added to my Mark Twain collection. I called George, agreed on a price, and mailed him a check.

I did not know much about photographs, but I knew I should be careful with them. The negatives arrived in groups wrapped in cardboard with rubberbands around them. I immediately went to a local photo shop to acquire sleeves for each of the negatives. The clerk sold me 4x5 inch transparent sleeves and I asked him whether they were of archival quality. He said he did not know and advised calling Customer Service at Eastman Kodak.

The following day I phoned one of the Eastman Kodak technicians who said the sleeves were not archival and suggested my getting in touch with someone from the International Museum of Photography at the George Eastman House in Rochester, New York. He also suggested, considering their age, that the negatives might be nitrate and therefore potentially explosive and highly flammable. My concerns grew. Late that afternoon I called Ruth Cook at Fort Wayne's Lincoln Museum to see if she had any information on nitrate negatives, and in her usual prompt manner she pulled some materials for me to read.

At home that evening I read the information and began placing each of the negatives in a transparent sleeve so that all could be examined carefully. One or two of the negatives were larger than the 4x5 inches, so a small excess was trimmed so that nothing was taken away from the original picture. The following day I lit one of those excess strips in a metal ash tray, and it burned like the fuse of a firecracker. The negatives were nitrate and unstable, to say the least.

The next step was to contact the George Eastman House in Rochester. Grant Romer, a conservator at the museum, spoke to me. He gave me excellent information about nitrate negatives. My immediate concern was about the possibility of fire or explosion, although the negatives had survived approximately ninety years. Grant assured me, "You have not brought a Trojan horse into your home." He concluded the conversation by stating that Michael Hager, the nitrate negative expert, would be available the following day.

The next day I contacted Michael at the museum. We discussed my find at length and what ought to be done about preserving the negatives. Nitrate film breaks down chemically and releases gases that accelerate its own decomposition. The by-products of the breakdown attack and destroy the gelatin and silver in the emulsion. High temperature and humidity are two other factors which accelerate the deterioration. It is remarkable that these negatives survived this long. Michael said that a duplicate set of negatives was imperative. He stated that he would submit a proposal for making the duplicate set of negatives and some prints on 8x10 archival paper from the original negatives. Several days later the proposal arrived. It looked good but expensive. Since my purpose was to do this project well, and knowing Michael to be one of the best, I hired him to do the job. Concerned about shipping the negatives to Michael because of the heat during the late summer, we decided to make some arrangements at a mutually agreeable time and place where he would receive the negatives.

Meanwhile in August I sent Mark Twain scholar Alan Gribben, in Austin, Texas, a photocopy of the manuscript, the prints, and a description of each of the negatives from which prints had not yet been made. I wanted his opinion about the potential for publication. Alan agreed that we had the potential for a book.

On a weekend in October Michael Hager and I met in Hudson, Ohio. The one hundred twenty-five nitrate negatives were given to him and he confirmed our agreement to make a duplicate set of negatives and three sets of prints from the original nitrate negatives. In December of 1984, Michael sent me photographs on five different types of papers to select for printing. After consultation with Alan and my friend Mark Neely, director of the Lincoln Museum, we determined that the prints needed to be made on Ektalure archival paper.

Four more negatives from the July-August 1895 trip were offered to me in July, 1985 by Gary Oleson, proprietor of Waiting For Godot Books in Cambridge, Massachusetts. After confirming that these four belonged with the trip group, I paid Gary and sent them off to Michael Hager for "processing." The negatives now numbered one hundred twenty-nine. Only eighteen of them had been previously published.

In August 1986, George Minkoff contacted me once again about some more Pond materials. In this lot was a forty-nine page typed unpublished manuscript written in 1948. It is entitled "Mark Twain's Other Trade" by James B. Pond, Jr., Major Pond's son. Referring to the 1895 trip, the manuscript states, "Father, having at last pushed the Clemens family off on its way to Australia, came home. He was bubbling over with tales of the tour. He presented me with the pipe Mark Twain had held in his teeth until the pipe had fallen somewhere and its meerschaum bowl been cracked beyond repair, at least for any practical smoking purposes."

The manuscript also tells about Mark Twain's annual summer workplace—Quarry Farm, stating, "There 'Bim' Pond, as I was known, played at Quarry Farm with Susy and Jean Clemens, the two daughters who had been left at home with Aunt Sue when their father and mother and sister Clara had gone off on the world jaunt. There was also a huge St. Bernard dog, quite as big as I was. He terrified me, even though I grew to love him." The pictures from Quarry Farm in this book show family and friends, including Osmon, the dog.

Also in this lot of Pond materials was a page of the Major's manuscript. The page included Mark Twain's acknowledgement of receipt of a group of these Quarry Farm pictures. Writing from Calcutta, India, on February 8, 1896 Twain told Pond: "Yes, indeed we got the Farm pictures and were delighted, and mama has written you, but goodness knows when you will get the letter. They made us very homesick and I feel farther away than ever. I wonder if we shall ever see America again. I hope so. The world never seemed so big before. But I am glad to be in it."

Introduction
by Alan Gribben

"I've a notion to read a few times in America before I sail for Australia."
(Mark Twain to James B. Pond, Paris, 1 May 1895)

"Writing is too slow for the demands that I have to meet; therefore I have begun to lecture my way around the world."
(Mark Twain, quoted by Samuel E. Moffett, San Francisco *Examiner*, 17 August 1895)

Mark Twain's global lecture tour of 1895–96 was a monumental undertaking even in terms of the eventful life he led, and it made an immense impression on the world press and his millions of admirers. It would be the longest of many sightseeing journeys for Twain, and his final series of paid platform performances. That this was in all likelihood his last tour made every appearance especially memorable for him and for his audiences, as well as for those who thronged to glimpse him pass along the way; the aging humorist was selling the world its few remaining opportunities to see him in person, and large numbers on successive continents queued up for the privilege of witnessing one of these historic occasions.

But this bittersweet sense of visiting towns and cities and certain people for the last time, as it were, understandably had a sobering effect on Twain and his entourage. The photographs that survive, greatly supplemented by those reproduced here for the first time, typically lack the carefree, insouciant atmosphere of pictures documenting his earlier tours; rather, a forced, determined air prevails, contrasting with Twain's initial hopes for some measure of jovial diversion from the trip. To a degree, no doubt, he was simply demonstrating his lifelong conviction (shared by most people of his generation) that "a photograph is a most important document, and there is nothing more damning to go down to posterity than a silly, foolish smile caught and fixed forever." [1] Still, the tense faces of Clemens, his wife Olivia, and their daughter Clara seem positively *world*–weary—as well they might, considering the exhausting pace of their travel, the endless greeting and smiling and lecturing, and the unpredictable comforts of

dining and lodging in the 1890's. Their facial expressions, and those of their companions, appear resolutely controlled and mutually supportive, but rarely relaxed or pleasurably engaged. Except for a few incidents of staged horseplay, like James B. Pond's pushing Twain about the railway station at Crookston, Minnesota, on a baggage truck, and in spite of the genial presence of Mrs. Pond during the journey from the railway station in Elmira, New York, to the ocean wharf at Victoria, British Columbia, Major Pond's camera shutter usually clicked open to portray a tired but dutiful Clemens trio.

The circumstances behind this tour, of course, scarcely could encourage much hope of delight in its progress. Publicly humiliated by the financial failures of his two principal business ventures—a publishing firm and a typesetting machine—followed by his personal bankruptcy in January 1895, Twain had agreed to the details of a demanding lecture tour while still reeling from these double blows of fiscal disappointment. The severe national Panic of 1893, a fatal casualness about selecting new titles for Charles L. Webster & Company to publish, a changing market for subscription-book sales, an unfortunate tendency to delegate vital business decisions but interfere in minor matters, a stubborn gambler's hunch to throw good money after bad in trying to develop the first typesetting machine, an insatiable yearning for more money than he or any author could earn by writing alone—these and other proclivities suddenly combined to identify Samuel L. Clemens as an embarrassed borrower of his wife's family funds and of large sums from their personal friends. Surely an extensive tour of artistic performances has seldom been commenced under less auspicious, more excruciating conditions.

In a sense, even so, the trip would conclude by worsening Twain's misery; in England on August 18, 1896 he would be handed a cable containing the soul-wrenching news that his beloved daughter Susy had died of meningitis. As he confirmed this ghastly fact and learned the pitiful details, Twain underwent a massive, grief-induced alteration in his personality that no amount of ensuing fame or financial security could ever effectually mitigate.

Yet there is another, more satisfying way to look at this tour, particularly the first leg of it, than as an agonizing prelude to disaster and tragedy. Twain's response to the calamity that his improvidence had brought upon himself and his family was, after all, genuinely ennobling. His prompt acquiescence to the idea of falling back on a gigantic version of his infallible stock in trade, the lecture circuit, to help erase his almost hopeless burden of debt is, as commentators of his day pointed out, comparable to the heroism displayed by a writer Twain claimed to detest, Sir Walter Scott, who valiantly strove to repay debts incurred in the bankruptcy of a publishing firm. One also thinks of Ulysses S. Grant, who took Twain's advice and invested the last painful months of his life in hoarsely dictating his battle memoirs in order to leave his family provided for. Moreover, Twain rallied his little touring party, and tried to keep up the spirits of his separated family, writing cheerfully to his daughters Susy and Jean in Elmira, and joshing with Livy and Clara in the carriages, on the trains, and on the ships that transported them about the stretches of the earth. It was, without question, Mark Twain's most sustained, difficult, and commendable performance. If he had been foolish in squandering his earnings, he was at least self-sacrificing and emphatically cheerful in making an effort to replace those lost hundreds of thousands of dollars. The man who once feared the prospect of being viewed as a mere literary "comedian" now found himself resembling, of necessity, a desperate pantaloon with a fixed smile as he responded to newspaper interviewers and sought out paying audiences in either hemisphere.

Still, the realities of the trip were not totally discouraging, whatever Twain anticipated. Here, Major James B. Pond's observations are especially revealing, because he and his wife accompanied Twain on the initial part of the tour, when the ache of separation from two of his three daughters was still fresh, when the public disgrace of his creditors' efforts to attach his remaining assets stung smartly, when he struggled to find and redevelop the dormant powers of stage presence he had once taken for granted, when he was traveling across his own nation but through an often sparsely populated region he had never before seen, and when the daunting prospect of continuous ocean and railway journeys lay uninvitingly before him. Yet during this early portion of the trip he seemingly recovered some of his equilibrium, discovered and reworked effective lecture materials, convinced Livy and Clara of the feasibility (or at least inevitability) of the tour, and took heart from the press notices and swelling crowds that began to make his tour seem triumphant and vindicating instead of nightmarish and begging.

Pond, the trusted old friend who had managed the Mark Twain-George Washington Cable tour of 1884–85, was there at Twain's side during every phase of this five-week struggle, and Pond's pen and camera worked daily to record the tremendous endeavor on Twain's part to overcome ill health, anxiety, and despair. The photographs and text that Nick Karanovich came into possession of in 1984 are therefore a rare and most inspiring literary and biographical treasure.

The camera recording this historic journey was the box-shaped novelty introduced by George Eastman in 1888 with an ingenious advertising slogan—"You press the button, we do the rest"—that helped its sales soar. Like the boom in video camera recorders a century later, new technological developments had abruptly made available a new, instant method for Americans to memorialize a particular family occasion, public event, or moment of whimsy. By 1895, in fact, Pond's personal penchant for taking snapshots was virtually a national pastime as well, and he and his fellow "Kodakers" eagerly mailed their film to Rochester, New York, for processing. In combining picture-taking with travel, however, Pond was in the vanguard rather than following a trend. As Susan Sontag has observed, "Photography develops in tandem with one of the most characteristic of modern activities: tourism.…Photographs will offer indisputable evidence that the trip was made, that the program was carried out, that fun was had.…The very activity of taking pictures is soothing, and assuages general feelings of disorientation that are likely to be exacerbated by travel.…This gives shape to experience: stop, take a photograph, and move on." [2] Even at the end of their overland journey, when Twain lay abed in Vancouver with a bad cold, Pond's Kodak (which Twain referred to as "his cartridge box") focused on the scene of newspaper reporters interviewing the ailing author. [3]

How Pond came to be Twain's chronicler on this transcontinental trip has as much to do with events in American cultural history in the previous decades as with Twain's distressed situation in 1895. James Burton Pond (1838–1903), a Civil War veteran only three years younger than Twain, was a relatively well-known figure in the second half of the nineteenth century. He and his predecessor, James Redpath (1833–1891), very likely did more to revolutionize the system of booking prominent authors and heroes for speaking engagements than any personages before or since.

When the New York City journalist and former abolitionist Redpath came upon the scene, Ralph Waldo Emerson lectured for as little as five dollars a night and community groups negotiated individually with him and other eminent speakers. Redpath established the Redpath Lyceum Bureau in Boston in 1868, charging a ten percent fee for his services and negotiating vastly improved contracts for the speakers he represented. Controversial figures like suffragette Anna E. Dickinson became a staple of his offerings.

Another female reformer launched James Pond's career as a lecture manager; Ann Eliza Young, Brigham Young's rebellious twenty-seventh wife, began divorce proceedings while Pond was a newspaperman for the Salt Lake City *Tribune*. His skillful management of her subsequent lectures against polygamy in 1874 soon led Pond to become associated with the Redpath Lecture Bureau. In 1875, Redpath sold his agency to Pond and a man named George H. Hathaway, who purchased Pond's interest four years later. Pond established his own agency in New York City in 1880. Among many others who joined his venerable list of speakers were Charles Sumner, besmirched minister Henry Ward Beecher (in 1876), Arthur Conan Doyle, James Whitcomb Riley, and explorer Henry M. Stanley. Pond assiduously cultivated Mark Twain, even during fallow years when Twain was indifferent to the enticements of lecturing, and Pond's promotional letterhead stationery on which he addressed letters to Twain frequently touted "Henry Ward Beecher's Lectures" or "Geo. W. Cable's Readings from His Own Works." [4] A letter from Pond to Twain written on 26 November 1890 beneath a letterhead advertising "Stanley's Am. Tour, Under the Direction of Maj. J. B. Pond," invites the Clemenses to come to New York City to hear Stanley talk on December 4th. "We are sweeping the country....Mr. Stanley is an Angel without wings." [5] When Mark Twain's financial peril became public, Pond wrote sympathetically and supportively: "I hope your business troubles will not break you down....The loss of a fortune is tough. There are other resources for another fortune & besides the abundant happiness and delight you have brought to every English speaking household where there is intelligence." [6]

Small wonder, then, that Mark Twain selected Pond as his American agent, or that he allowed Pond to make (and later publish) a record of that part of the journey. Pond's brother Ozias, in fact, had kept a diary between January and April 1885 that contained many references to the reading tour of Twain and Cable he was accompanying; James B. Pond's notes are recognizable in this document. [7] Pond himself is an underestimated writer, as a glance at his "A Pioneer Boyhood: Recollections of the West in the Forties" (1899) will confirm. [8] In richly evocative prose, he gives an account of his move as a young boy from New York state to rural Illinois and thence to Fond du Lac County, Wisconsin—memories of boy-life on a primitive farm that are, in many passages, the equal of Hamlin Garland's autobiographical *Boy Life on the Prairie* (1899). "I found every line of your boyhood article in the magazine well said & interesting," Twain wrote. [9] Pond's earlier essay, "The Lyceum" (1896), [10] calls Anna E. Dickinson "the 'Queen of the Lyceum' " and observes that "the intellectual character of the lyceum entertainments has been gradually falling....Of late our people have had so much to read about and to talk about that even heroes [of Antarctic exploration] are common" (600-602). He attributes the decline of the lyceum to more attractive theaters and to improvements in newspaper production that have enabled them to report on "almost everything to be said on the subjects of progress, genius, education, reform, and entertainment" (601). Pond's background in journalism and his habit of making business memoranda endowed him with a flexible, observant style that is evident in these writings and in his treatments of the Twain tour of 1895.

James B. Pond and Samuel L. Clemens had curious parallels and striking differences in their biographical backgrounds, and both seemed to draw them closer together. Pond came from a family of eleven children, and grew up in a log-house that probably resembled Clemens' birthplace in Florida, Missouri. At the age of fourteen Pond left home to learn the printing craft, and worked in printing offices and for newspapers as an itinerant journeyman printer, much as Clemens did. He was a newspaper editor and publisher in a small town in Wisconsin when the Civil War erupted, and soon became a commissioned officer in the Third Wisconsin cavalry. His regiment was stationed for several years on the border of Kansas and Missouri, and in October 1863 Pond's regiment was nearly decimated by the guerrilla force of William Quantrill, which donned Federal uniforms and showed the Union flag to gain access to Pond's camp at Baxter Springs, Kansas, following Quantrill's deadly assault on Lawrence, Kansas. With only a handful of survivors, Pond managed to hold the camp until reinforcements arrived. In 1864 Pond was commissioned as a major, a title he (like many Civil War veterans) elected to retain in civilian life. Clemens' fascination with the military figures such as General Grant who had witnessed the horrors of a conflict Clemens himself evaded is well known; here is another instance of a close personal friendship that seemed enhanced rather than hindered by Pond's bloody experiences in the Missouri-Kansas region. Pond's first wife, whom he married in 1859, died in 1871 in Leavenworth, Kansas. They had one daughter. In 1888 he married Martha Marion Glass of Jersey City, New Jersey, who is the pert-looking "Mrs. Pond" identifiable in many of Pond's snapshots from the trip to Vancouver. Their only child, young James Burton ("Bim") Pond, Jr. (1889–1961), would recall that his parents "left me in Jersey City with my Grandmother" when they joined the Clemenses for "a trip across the American Continent with the famous Mark. Letters and souvenir cards drifted back to me." [11] The boy does not appear in his father's photographs until the Ponds were reunited with him and returned to Quarry Farm.

Mark Twain scarcely made any use of the North American segment of his lecture tour in *Following the Equator* (1897), merely mentioning at the beginning of chapter one that "we started westward from New York in midsummer, with Major Pond to manage the platform-business as far as the Pacific. It was warm work, all the way....We sailed at last; and so ended a snail-paced march across the continent, which had lasted forty days." [12] None of Pond's snapshots went into Twain's book, either. Presumably Twain decided that descriptions of domestic and Canadian travel might dilute the exotic appeal of his "foreign" experiences. In Clara Clemens' subsequent account, too, the overland trip is only briefly characterized as "a triumphal march across the continent of America. Each city turned out to welcome my father in great numbers and with such vehemently expressed cordiality that he soon got into the spirit of his task." [13] Twain's notebook for 1895, on the other hand, logged his impressions during the trip, such as his reverie about the vast stretches of wheat fields though which the train passed: "There is the peace of the ocean about it and a deep contentment, a heaven-wide sense of ampleness, spaciousness." [14]

James B. Pond also set down the details of the trip, even noting, in Crookston, Minnesota, that their party of five people traveled with sixteen pieces of hand baggage. Pond, however, departed from his companions in

subsequently employing his journal for multiple publications. The manuscript acquired by Nick Karanovich in 1984 constitutes an original, fuller version of the account of Twain's tour that Pond partially published in 1900 in four forms. [15] The version appearing in Pond's *Eccentricities of Genius: Memories of Famous Men and Women of the Platform and Stage* (1900), replete with two of Pond's snapshots, is the most complete of these four, but none, as it turns out, is so frank or detailed as the Karanovich manuscript. [16] Twain's letters written en route corroborate and expand upon Pond's deductions about his lecturer's emotional state. "Thus far I have had more people in three opera houses than they've ever had in them before, winter or summer; and they swelter there with admirable patience," Twain boasted to his wealthy financial advisor, Henry H. Rogers, on July 29th from Crookston, Minnesota. "You *must* hire a private car some day and take a swing through this splendid country," he added enthusiastically. [17] Together with such letters, Twain's personal notebook, and scattered newspaper interviews, [18] Pond's records make up most of what we know about the crucial initiating weeks of the tour of 1895.

The document purchased by Mr. Karanovich consists of ninety-three typed pages that are numbered in several sequences; many pages of the typescript contain Pond's interlinear or marginal additions and cancellations in ink. In places Pond also interleaved handwritten sheets of supplemental narrative. Nearly a quarter of this total manuscript, which derives, Pond said in *Eccentricities of Genius*, from "a detailed journal," never appeared in Pond's book. At intervals in the typescript Pond inserted related materials he evidently prepared at other times, including an account of his visit to Quarry Farm with his wife and child in September 1895 and a transcript of Mark Twain's speech at the first production of *Pudd'nhead Wilson*.

Although Pond's *Eccentricities of Genius*—a collection of generally flattering portraits of famous speakers who put themselves under his management—reproduces the larger part of his original draft narrating Twain's tour, he pulled back from some of his most candid comments about the communities and audiences they encountered. For the historical record, it is good to have this broader access to the earlier manuscript. What we mainly lost in reading only the previously published versions of Pond's account were the more extreme reactions of disappointment or surprise on

Pond's part, along with incidental facts as well as revelatory calculations about the profits (or losses) of various "houses" that Twain drew. Here we learn, for example, that Twain ignored a Mr. Chute at dinner in Minneapolis and then grew contrite and sent a letter of apology; that the hotel in Crookston, Minnesota, was so new that an electrician had to illuminate and adjust the lights in their room; that Pond felt disgust upon learning that the hotel proprietors in Butte, Montana, "charge us $5.00 a day each, and the extortions from porters, baggage-men, and bell-boys, surpass anything I ever heard of." In a section that Pond subsequently canceled, he lashes out at the theater management in Great Falls, Montana: "No one here that knows about the business. No notices in the papers; no one seems to know or care about our coming. The first time there has been no advance sale. Receipts of evening were only $220.50. We get 70% of that." The previously published versions are perhaps more polished, but most readers will probably prefer the candor of this edition with its occasional glimpses of Pond confiding, gloating, or feeling indignant. His narrative was the poorer for omitting, in the published versions of 1900, the story of how, for the satisfaction of reaping an even sum of $400 from an audience in Mackinac (after he had already collected $398), Pond persuaded two young, wavering late-comers to fork over a dollar apiece for admission upon the promise that after the show he would introduce them to Mark Twain and take them down to the billiard room for drinks—a pledge he kept. Differences in the versions are often textually minor, but these intermittent variants help to assure us readers that in the Karanovich manuscript Pond is a more reliable narrator who withholds little that is significant.

All of the versions mention Twain's "sick bed" condition at the outset of the tour, and his "improving" status as the weeks pass and Twain endures the zigzag itinerary of more than twenty cities that Pond arranged for him in an immense, upward-sweeping arc beginning with a premiere performance in Cleveland. [19] The disappointing lecture audiences of Anaconda and Helena, Montana, and Spokane, Washington, are compensated for by the grand welcomes waiting for Twain in Portland, Oregon, and Olympia, Washington. A reporter in Portland sketched the celebratory scene as Twain and Pond stood outside their hotel after the lecture: "Dozens of people" endeavored "to reach over the array of handbags and shake hands with Mark Twain. Most of them claimed to have met him before....That genial courteous gentleman, Major J. B. Pond, was busy with introductions and other matters." The Portland reporter thought Mark Twain was "certainly about as striking and picturesque a character as ever looked out of the pages of any of his own books." Indeed, with "the originality of his manner, its absolute carelessness, its lazy, cynical good humor, he becomes one of the most interesting men in the world to meet." According to this reporter, "a blue nautical cap confined a part of his big mane of hair, but it bulged out at the sides and behind, a grizzly wilderness." Twain paused to praise Portland as "a pretty nice town....I haven't had an opportunity to see much of Portland, because, through the diabolical machinations of Major Pond over there, I am compelled to leave it after but a glimpse. I may never see Portland again, but I liked that glimpse," he said. [20]

In Vancouver, British Columbia, "a fine audience" revived Twain from his exhaustion, and a few days later, at the conclusion of Pond's section of the trip, Twain presented him with a copy of *Roughing It* bearing a warm inscription: "To J. B. Pond/from his friend/The Author./In memory of the pleasant platform campaign of July & August, 1895,/Victoria, B. C., Aug. 22/95". [21] Twain wound up this American part of the tour, however, with a bad sore throat and cold, and his mood at the time seemed in keeping with the gloomy scene along the coast; forest fires were devastating portions of the Washington wilderness, and a pall of dense smoke stretched from Tacoma to Vancouver. Grimly he informed Henry H. Rogers that "the smoke is so dense all over this upper coast that you can't see a cathedral at 800 yards." [22] As Twain and his family left Victoria aboard the *Warrimoo* (which would run aground trying to clear the harbor), "we waved to one another as long as they kept in sight," Pond recalled, and he took several final photographs. He had fulfilled his demanding obligations as the United States manager for his client, and now he watched the Clemenses pass out of sight with misgivings about Twain's physical afflictions and his "perpetual smoking." Pond doubtless intuited the many honors and misadventures that lay ahead of his friends in Australia, India, South Africa, and other nations. [23] Returning to the railroad depot, Pond and his wife Martha retraced much of the just–completed lecture route going eastward, and, after rejoining their little boy "Bim," visited the Clemens daughters at Quarry Farm outside Elmira, New York. Pond's Kodak camera was kept busy on the premises of that hillside retreat, partly to reassure the parents of Susy and Jean that they were enjoying their stay at the home of Theodore and Susan Crane, where they had spent so many childhood summers.

None of Pond's later efforts could induce Mark Twain to return to the platform again. Their correspondence, much of it excerpted in *Eccentricities of Genius*, suggests how diligently Pond tried to change Twain's mind. In 1897 he reminded Pond that "I was never very well, from the first night in Cleveland to the last one in Cape Town....I did a good deal of talking when I ought to have been in bed.... I...am not going to allow myself to think of London, or any other platform, for a long time to come." [24] He repeated this assertion more humorously on March 15, 1898: "Lecturing? No, I was intending to lecture in Austria and around about but when I got out of debt I cancelled all that. Honest people do not go robbing the public on the platform, except when they are in debt." [25] On April 4, 1899, he explained: "I like to talk for nothing, about twice a year; but talking for money is *work*, and that takes the pleasure out of it. I do not believe you could offer me terms that would dissolve my prejudice against the platform. I do not expect to see a platform again until the wolf commands." [26] Still, Pond persisted in dangling attractive terms, and Twain replied to one proposition on September 1, 1899: "A thousand dollars a night is plenty good enough pay and I thank you for the compliment of the offer, but I do not like the platform and will not lecture so long as I can earn a living in honest ways." [27] This bantering would continue for years; on October 30, 1902, Twain reiterated: "I would strain several points for you but I wouldn't go on the platform and bring down another avalanche of invitations for the best $50,000 in America. I shall never read or lecture again, except in a private house." [28]

Thus the commercial relationship of Pond and his famous speaker shifted back to its alternate mode of social calls and letters. Pond would never again receive the enthusiastic missives that came to him from Twain in the 1870's, 1880's, and 1890's about the immense possibilities for enriching themselves through astute managing of his lecturing dates. He must have held hopes for another letter like the one from Twain that had arrived on May 1, 1895: "I've a notion to read a few times in America before I sail for Australia. I'm going to think it over and make up my

mind." [29] Pond then hurriedly arranged an itinerary of twenty-two engagements, eventually deciding against San Francisco, the site of Twain's first lecture, in favor of sticking to an East-West route along the Canadian border. For that brief time of urgent financial need in 1895, Twain summoned up his former energies and implored Pond to stress, in circulars for his "campaign," that Mark Twain "*is on his way to Australia and thence around the globe on a reading and talking tour to last 12 months. You get the idea? Traveling around the world is nothing. Everybody does it. What I am traveling for* [to deliver a series of lectures] *is unusual. Everybody doesn't do that.*" [30] Pond complied with respect to this and other pieces of Twain's advice, and the result was a tour that Twain had few complaints about, other than his health and the overriding reason he was compelled to conceive of such an arduous "campaign" in the first place.

Granting a newspaper interview to his nephew Samuel E. Moffett, for example, Twain expressed satisfaction that "in my preliminary run through the smaller cities on the northern route I have found a reception the cordiality of which has touched my heart and made me feel how small a thing money is in comparison with friendship." On the other hand, he explained that "I do not enjoy the hard travel and broken rest inseparable from lecturing, and if it had not been for the imperious moral necessity of paying these debts...I should never have taken to the road at my time of life. I could have supported myself comfortably by writing, but writing is too slow for the demands that I have to meet; therefore I have begun to lecture my way around the world." [31]

There were other conspicuous benefits of the tour besides the remunerative reuniting of a celebrated literary artist and his former lecture manager. Twain's travel narrative of the ensuing journey, *Following the Equator* (1897), while never ranked among his best productions, nevertheless contains a number of riveting passages and in its close examination of a traveler's cultural values and prejudices helped prepare the way for modern travel writers like Paul Theroux. Conceivably Pond's ubiquitous Kodaking (a neologism that the stylistic purist Twain could never accept as a verb) [32] encouraged Twain's decision to include photographic illustrations of foreign scenes in the text of *Following the Equator*—though it should be recognized that this practice of incorporating photographs in published travel narratives had its beginnings in the 1850's [33] and that none of

Pond's snapshots appeared in Twain's book. There is now another, more tangible bonus of the tour to consider: James B. Pond's enlightening record of the first segment of the journey, written with modesty and discernment and total engagement. The slangy tone that Pond adopts—"nearly knocked 'Mark' off his pins," "Mark was simply immense," "I took the risk outside, and won"—gradually becomes winsome; the Pond persona here seems so trustworthy, so close to the moment of jotting down the impression, as to avoid that tendency of Twain's designated biographer Albert Bigelow Paine (the better writer, no doubt) to feel obliged to evaluate every experience and make it fit neatly within the matrix of a larger pattern of conduct. Quickened perhaps by the hurtling railway coaches in which he was a passenger, Pond's pace, too, is brisk and straightforward; no amateurish amassing of extraneous details mars this narrative.

Pond's ulterior motive, if any, is simply to bring us to the point of agreeing with his concluding opinion that, since "business relations and travelling bring out the nature of a man," accordingly he has ample justification to pronounce Twain not only a genius but "a sympathetic, honest, brave gentleman." The latter word no longer possesses specific connotations it called forth in Pond's day, but the reader of this chronicle will nonetheless encounter vivid and likeable dimensions of Mark Twain's personality in these pages. There is every reason to be grateful that this manuscript and the illustrating photographs have entered into Mr. Karanovich's collection, and that he is making them available in a complete edition. This book depicts Mark Twain as he appeared when besieged and discouraged, but the image of the man (and his family) is still immensely appealing. Nearly a century after Twain chuckled and quipped bravely through his ordeal, the publication of this typescript memoir and its documenting photographs provides the means for a fresh appreciation of admirable personal and professional qualities in the figure who contributed so substantially to the colloquial voice in American literature.

Notes

1. Quoted by Elizabeth Wallace, *Mark Twain and the Happy Island* (Chicago: A. C. McClurg & Co, 1913), p. 34.

2. Susan Sontag, *On Photography* (New York: Farrar, Straus and Giroux, 1977), pp. 9-10. For historical documentation concerning the phenomenon of American snapshots, see such articles as Robert E. Mensel's " 'Kodakers Lying in Wait': Amateur Photography and the Right of Privacy in New York, 1885–1915," *American Quarterly* 43 (March 1991): 24–45, esp. Notes 6, 22–31.

3. Vancouver *News–Advertiser*, August 21, 1895; quoted by Ruth Axtell Burnet in "Mark Twain in the Northwest, August 9–23, 1895," M. A. Thesis, University of Washington, 1950, p. 20. I am grateful to Thomas A. Tenney for calling my attention to this helpful study.

4. For instance, on an ALS, 16 February 1884, Mark Twain Project, Bancroft Library, University of California, Berkeley.

5. *The Twainian*, September–October 1976, 35: 3.

6. Jersey City, 19 April 1894; ALS in Mark Twain Project at Berkeley.

7. Henry W. and Albert A. Berg Collection, New York Public Library, Astor, Lenox and Tilden Foundations.

8. *Century Magazine* 58 (October 1899): 929–937.

9. Clemens to Pond, London, October 19, 1899 (Berg Collection, New York Public Library).

10. *Cosmopolitan* 20 (April 1896) : 595–602.

11. "Mark Twain's Other Trade," unpublished typescript, 1948, collection of Nick Karanovich, Fort Wayne, Indiana.

12. *Following the Equator: A Journey Around the World* (Hartford, CT.: American Publishing Co., 1897), p. 25.

13. Clara Clemens, *My Father, Mark Twain* (New York: Harper & Brothers, 1931), pp. 138–139.

14. Quoted by Albert Bigelow Paine, *Mark Twain: A Biography*, 2 vols. (New York: Harper & Brothers, 1912), p. 1003.

15. As a magazine article ("Across the Continent with Mark Twain," *Saturday Evening Post*, 29 September 1900, 6–7); as a brief newspaper article, "Mark Twain's Return from a Tour Around the Globe to Pay His Debts" (New York *Times*, 20 October 1900; as a small (eleven-page) pamphlet, *Mark Twain and General Grant: Major Pond's Tribute to the Great Humorist* (N. p., 1900?), in the collection of Kevin B. MacDonnell, Austin, Texas; and, in the version closest to the original source, as a book chapter in *Eccentricities of Genius: Memories of Famous Men and Women of the Platform and Stage* (New York: G. W. Dillingham Co., 1900), pp. 197-230.

16. Milton Meltzer reproduced one of these snapshots (of Pond pushing Twain on a baggage truck in Crookston) and nine others taken by Pond in *Mark Twain Himself: A Pictorial Biography* (Hannibal, Missouri: Becky Thatcher Book Shop, 1960), pp. 225-229. The other picture that Pond employed in *Eccentricities of Genius* was a photograph of all five travelers on the deck of the *Warrimoo*, obligingly taken by another passenger.

17. *Mark Twain's Correspondence with Henry Huttleston Rogers 1893–1901*, ed. Lewis Leary (Berkeley: University of California Press, 1969), p. 177.

18. Conveniently listed and partially reprinted in Louis J. Budd, "A Listing of and Selection from Newspaper and Magazine Interviews with Samuel L. Clemens, 1874–1910," *American Literary Realism* 10 (Winter 1977): 1–100.

19. See also, in this connection, Fred W. Lorch, "Mark Twain's 'Morals' Lecture During the American Phase of the World Tour in 1895–1896," *American Literature* 26 (March 1954): 52–66; and Lorch, *The Trouble Begins at Eight: Mark Twain's Lecture Tours* (Ames: Iowa State University Press, 1968), 183–210.

20. Lute Pease, Portland *Oregonian*, 11 August 1895, p. 10; reprinted in *Critical Essays on Mark Twain, 1867–1910*, ed. Louis J. Budd (Boston: G. K. Hall & Co., 1982), pp. 106–107.

21. C. Waller Barrett Collection, Univ. of Virginia at Charlottesville; photocopy of inscription in MTP. The Ponds evidently received two inscribed copies of *Roughing It*, since Pond's journal for August 16th quotes another, more fulsome inscription.

22. *Mark Twain's Correspondence with Henry Huttleston Rogers*, p. 186.

23. One phase of the tour is examined by Miriam Jones Shillingsburg, *At Home Abroad: Mark Twain in Australasia* (Jackson: University Press of Mississippi, 1988.)

24. *Eccentricities of Genius*, pp. 225–226. Although he initially objected to Pond's intention to quote from their correspondence in *Eccentricities of Genius* (Clemens to Pond, 14 September 1900, Berg Collection), Mark Twain ultimately consented to that proposal and praised Pond's book as "well written & distinctly interesting" (Clemens to Pond, 3 December 1900, Berg Collection).

25. Typescript copy in collection of Nick Karanovich; original ALS in Berg Collection, New York Public Library.
26. *Eccentricities of Genius*, p. 226.
27. Typescript copy in collection of Nick Karanovich; original ALS in Berg Collection, New York Public Library.
28. Typescript copy in collection of Nick Karanovich; original ALS in Berg Collection, New York Public Library.
29. *Eccentricities of Genius*, p. 200.
30. *Eccentricities of Genius*, p. 200, corrected from typescript copy in collection of Nick Karanovich; original ALS in Berg Collection, New York Public Library.
31. San Francisco *Examiner*, 17 August 1895, p. 2; reprinted in *Critical Essays on Mark Twain, 1867–1910*, p. 111.
32. Noted by John Seelye, *Mark Twain in the Movies: A Meditation with Pictures* (New York: Viking Press, 1977), p. 124.
33. See, for example, Stephen White, "The Photographically Illustrated Book," *A B Bookman's Weekly* 67 (January 12, 1981): 163–178; and Neil Harris, "Pictorial Perils: The Rise of American Illustration," in *The American Illustrated Book in the Nineteenth Century*, ed. Gerald W. R. Ward (Winterthur, Delaware: Henry Francis du Pont Winterthur Museum, 1987), pp. 11–19.

Textual Note
by Alan Gribben

Either James B. Pond or an assistant typed this present document as a draft of what Pond would publish about Mark Twain in *Eccentricities of Genius* (1900). Pond then made numerous revisions and additions in black ink. The typescript and interlineations have been followed in this transcription, except that obvious typographical errors ("but" accidentally typed as "hut," "not" rendered as "mot") are emended. Cancellations are not recorded unless they seem significant for purposes of understanding Pond's intentions in specific passages; such deletions are reported within angle brackets.

In one portion of Pond's report of the tour, he introduced handwritten pages of manuscript (numbered 19–24) that are in some places difficult to decipher despite his effort to write legibly in ink. There are a few other instances in which he added a handwritten page of manuscript, as with the page he numbered 30A—his description of Mark Twain's berating a ship captain. Another person's hand, possibly Mrs. Pond's, contributed three sentences, two of them about Quarry Farm. All of these holograph extensions have been transcribed and included with as much accuracy as possible. Beginning on the page numbered 19, an account of Twain's and Pond's arrival in Portland, Pond signaled a series of insertions of various passages by marking them and their intended positions with the capital letters "H" through "M"; his stipulated sequence (not alphabetical in order) has been followed in this edition.

Ampersands are rendered as "and" throughout, since the typescript routinely made this conversion. In cases of duplication of sentences (either handwritten or typed), the editorial practice is to follow Pond's final wording, as determined by textual evidence and comparison with published versions, and to omit repeated material unless it differs more substantially than in incidental structure or minor phrasing. Pond's inadvertent lapses in spelling, punctuation, and other matters of grammar have been allowed to stand.

The editors have supplied a title for Pond's record of the tour: *Overland with Mark Twain*. Section headings derive from Pond's typescript.

Overland with Mark Twain: James B. Pond's Journal

Mark Twain.

S. L. Clemens (Mark Twain) I consider one of the greatest geniuses of our time, and as great a philosopher as a humorist. I think I know him better than most men do,—universal as his circle of acquaintance is,—big as is his reputation. He is as great a man as he is a genius, too. Tenderness and sensitiveness are his two strongest traits. He has one of the best hearts that ever beat. One must know him well to fully discern all of his best traits. He keeps them entrenched, so to speak. I rather imagine that he fights shy of having it generally suspected that he is kind and tender hearted, but many of his old friends do know it.

He possesses some of the frontier traits—a fierce spirit of retaliation, and the absolute confidence that life–long "partners," in the Western sense, develops. Injure him and he is merciless, especially if you betray his confidence. Once a lecture manager in New York, whom he trusted to arrange the details of a lecture in Steinway Hall, swindled him to the amount of some $1,500. and afterwards confessed it, offering restitution to that amount, that being Mark's share of the plunder, but not until it had been discovered. They were on board ship at the time, and Mark threatened to throw the fellow overboard, and meant it, too, but he fled ashore. In "The Gilded Age," Mark immolates him. (Mr. Griller, Lecture Agent. Page 438, London Edition.) The fellow died soon afterwards, and James Redpath, who was a witness to the scene on the steamboat, and who knew the man well, insisted that "Mark's" arrow killed him, but he would have fired it all the same had he known what the result would be.

General Grant and Mark Twain were the greatest of friends. C. L. Webster & Co. (Mark Twain) published "General Grant's Memoirs." How like and yet unlike are the careers of the soldier and the citizen!

Grant: poor, a tanner, small farmer, selling cord–wood for a living, with less prospect for rising than any ex–West Pointer in the Army; then the biggest military reputation of the age; then twice President of the United States; then the foremost civilian of the world; then the most honored guest of peoples and rulers, who ever made the circuit of the earth.

Mark Twain: A printer's apprentice in a small Missouri River town; then a "tramping jour" printer; a Mississippi River roustabout guarding freight piles on the levee all night for pocket money; river pilot; a rebel guerilla; a reporter in a Nevada mining town; then suddenly the most famous author of the age; a man of society, with the most aristocratic clubs of America, and all around the civilized globe, flung open to him; adopted with all the honors into one of the most exclusive societies on this continent, the favored companion of the most cultivated spirits of the age, welcomed abroad in all the courts almost as a crowned head. "Peace hath its victories," etc., etc.

There is indeed quite a parallel between Grant and Twain. Grant found himself impoverished two years before his death, when was left for him the most heroic part of his life work, to write his memoirs (while he knew he was dying), which, through his publishers, C. L. Webster & Co. (Twain), netted his family nearly half a million dollars. That firm failed in 1894, leaving liabilities to the amount of $80,000. over and above all it owned, for Mark to pay, and which he has earned with his voice and pen in a tour around the world, and paid every creditor in full, in one year's less time than calculated by Mark when he started at Cleveland on the 15th day of July, 1895. Yes, there is a parallel between the two great heroes, in courage and integrity; they are more than unlike.

Across the Continent with Mark Twain.

"Mark Twain" first became a lecturer in California, in 1865. He had returned to San Francisco from the Sandwich Islands, from which he had written a series of picturesque and humorous letters for a California journal, and was asked to lecture about the Islands. He used to tell his first experience with great glee. He had written the lecture and committed it to memory, and was satisfied with it; still, he dreaded a failure on the first night, as he had had no experience in addressing audiences. Accordingly, he made an arrangement with a woman friend, whose family was to occupy one of the boxes, to start the applause if he should give the sign by looking in her direction and stroking his moustache. He thought that if he failed to "strike" the audience, he would be encouraged by a round of applause if any one would start it after he had made a good point.

Instead of failure, his lecture was a boundless success. The audience rapturously applauded every point, and "Mark" forgot all about his instructions to the lady. Finally, as he was thinking of some new point that occurred to him as he was talking, without thinking of the lady at all, he unconsciously put his hand up to his moustache, and happened to turn in the direction of the box. He had said nothing just then to cause even his appreciative audience to applaud, but the lady took his action for the signal, and nearly broke her fan in striking it against the edge of the box. The whole house joined her applause.

This unexpected and malapropos applause almost knocked "Mark" off his pins, but he soon recovered himself and became at once one of the favorites of the platform. He lectured a year or two in the West, just after the close of the war, but by Petroleum V. Nasby's advice in 1872–3, Redpath invited him to come East, and he made his first appearance in Boston in the Redpath Lyceum, Music Hall. His success was instantaneous, and he has remained the universal platform favorite to this date, not only in America, in Australia, in India, in the Cape Colonies, and throughout Great Britain, but in Austria and in Germany, where large crowds pay higher prices to see and to hear "Mark Twain" than any other private citizen that has ever lived.

In his Tour Around the World, Mark Twain earned, with his voice and pen, money enough to pay all his creditors in full with interest, and this he did almost a year sooner than he had originally calculated. Such a triumphal tour has never before been made by any American hero since that memorable Tour Around the World by General Grant. He has been greeted in France, Switzerland, Germany and England almost like a crowned head.

He wrote me from Paris, May 1st, 1895: "I've a notion to read a few times in America before I sail for Australia. I'm going to think it over and make up my mind".

On May 18th he arrived in this country, and I made arrangements for him to lecture in twenty–one cities on his way to the Pacific, beginning in Cleveland, July 15th, and ending in Vancouver, British Columbia, August 15th. From that place he was to sail for Australia, via Honolulu, where it was planned that he should speak while the ship was waiting, but owing to yellow fever no landing was made and over $1600. was returned to the disappointed Honoluluans.

June 11th, he wrote me from Elmira:

"If you've got to have a circular for this brief campaign, the chief feature, when speaking of me should be, that he, (M.T.) *is on his way to Australia and thence around the globe on a reading and talking tour to last twelve months.*

"You get the idea? Travelling *around the world* is nothing—everybody does it. But what I am travelling *for* is unusual—everybody doesn't do *that*.

"I like the approximate itinerary first rate. It is *lake*, all the way from Cleveland to Duluth. I wouldn't switch aside to Milwaukee for $200,000."

His original idea was to lecture in nine cities besides two or three others on the Pacific Coast. I was to have one fourth of the profits except in San Francisco, where he was to have four fifths. But we did not go to San Francisco. <Fargo was in the original itinerary also.>

Two days before he started from Elmira, N. Y., he had been dragged from a sick-bed to appear in New York City, in supplementary proceedings. I declare that never have I witnessed a more pathetic spectacle than this sick man, facing what seemed to be a merciless court and a still more heartless creditor, who owed more of his business success to his victim than to any other source. Mark did not complain, but silently left the court–room with fixed determination to work out his salvation and his freedom from debts,—a form of slavery more to be abhorred than any other in existence. For weeks he had been suffering from a malignant carbuncle of the most prodigious proportions.

There were five of us in the party, Mr. and Mrs. Clemens, Clara, one of their daughters, Mrs. Pond and I. During the journey, I kept a detailed journal, from which I shall quote.

Cleveland, July 15th, '95.

The Stillman—with "Mark Twain", his wife and their daughter, Clara. "Mark" looks badly fatigued. His huge carbuncle seven weeks old, and the annoying supplementary proceedings in New York are telling upon him.

Very comfortable quarters at The Stillman. "Mark" went immediately to bed on our arrival. He is nervous and weak. Threats of interference with his lecture business here by his one annoying creditor worries him, but he is nursed and cared for by his tender, affectionate wife, whose soothing influence on him seems instantaneous. Reporters from all the morning and evening papers called and interviewed him. It seemed like old times again, and "Mark" enjoyed it. The young men called at 3 P.M. and paid me the fee for the lecture, which took place in Music Hall. 4,200 people present at prices ranging from 25¢ to $1.00. It was nine o'clock before the crowd could get in and "Mark" begin. As he hobbled upon the stage there was a grand ovation of cheers and applause which continued for some time. Then he began to speak, and before he could finish a sentence, the applause broke out again. So it went on for over an hour, on a mid–July night, with the mercury trying to climb out of the top of the thermometer. "Mark Twain" kept that vast throng in convulsions.

Tuesday, July 16th.

90 degrees in the shade at 7:30 A.M. Cleveland. Good notices of "Mark Twain's" lecture in all the papers. "Mark" spent all day in bed until five o'clock. I spent the day in writing to all correspondents ahead. If Sault Ste Marie, the next engagement, turns out as well in proportion as this place, our tour is a success. "Mark" and family out to dinner with some old friends and companions of the Quaker City tour. He came home very nervous and much distressed. There are intimations that his baggage will be

attached and other annoyances. I can't help it. I feel that <this man and his wife> these people have surrendered all they have to their creditors, and <now> I don't believe the creditors think half as much of them as they would, had they taken care of themselves. <My heart aches for them both.> We discover a remarkable woman in Mrs. Clemens. A good time is in store for us all.

Wednesday, July 17th.

Mercury 98° degrees still on the ascent. S.S. Northland. Our party left Cleveland for Mackinac at seven o'clock. <"Mark" much debilitated.> He is carrying on a big fight against his bodily disability. All that has been said of this fine ocean ship on the Great Lakes is not exaggerated. There is an ice plant on board that produces five tons of ice daily, and an electric plant that supplies two thousand seven hundred incandescent burners. The trip across Lake Erie to Detroit River, Lake St. Clair and the St. Clair River is most charming. "Mark" and Mrs. Clemens are very cheerful to–day. The passengers have discovered who they are. Our party is the center of attraction. Wherever "Mark" sits or stands on the deck of the steamer, in the smoking room, dining room, or cabin, he is the magnet, and people strain their necks to see him and to catch every word he utters.

New Venice, on the St. Clair River, is a most interesting resort. I have seen nothing else like it in America. For miles on the American side are rows of cottages built upon piles over the water, with no means of communication with each other except by small row boats, and these are numerous. There is a little slip, or dock, with pretty boats and boat houses by every cottage. Some of the boats are very elaborate. This is a unique resort for wealthy people of Michigan, Ohio and Indiana, and quite a number of Chicagoans have elegant summer homes here. There is great opportunity for fishing and duck shooting, as the Canadian side of the river is a vast rice marsh inhabited by water fowls only. Now few eastern people know of these extensive luxurious resorts, and all the growth of two decades.

On the second day out on Lake Huron, "Mark" was on deck in the morning for the first time, feeling fresh and spry as a young kitten. Many people made excuses for speaking to him. One man had stopped off in

Cleveland on purpose to hear him. Another from Washington Territory, who had lived forty years in the West, owned a copy of "Roughing It," which he and his wife knew by heart. One very gentle elderly lady wished to thank him for the nice things he has written and said of cats. But the one who interested "Mark" the most was a young man who asked him if he had ever seen or used a shaving stone, handing him one. It was a small, peculiar, fine–grained sandstone, the shape of a miniature grindstone, and about the size of an ordinary watch. He explained that all you had to do was to rub your face with it and the rough beard would disappear, leaving a clean shaven face.

Mark took it, rubbed it on his unshaven cheek, and express[ed] great wonder at the result. He put it in his vest pocket very unceremoniously, remarking at the same time:

"That is just what I want. The Madam (he generally speaks of Mrs. Clemens as "The Madam") will have no cause to complain of my never being ready in time for church because it takes so long to shave. I will just put this into my vest pocket on Sunday. Then when I get to church, I'll pull the thing out and enjoy a quiet shave in my pew during the long prayer. I see it is called "Adam's S[h]aving Stone." Of course Adam had no other means of shaving, so he just laid his cheek on a stone and it became smooth."

Friday, July 19th, Mackinac, Grand Hotel.

We came by steamer T. S. Faxton, of the Arnold Line. It was an ideal excursion among the islands. It was cold, but none of our party would leave the deck until dinner bell rang. Mark said, "That sounds like an old fashioned summons to dinner. It means a good old fashioned unpretentious dinner, too. I'm going to try it." We all sat down to a table reaching the entire length of the cabin. We naturally fell in with the rush and all got seats. It was a good dinner, too—the best I ever heard of for 25 cents. At 4:30 we reached the Grand Hotel, where I saw one of Mark's lithographs in the hotel office, and "Tickets For Sale Here" written in blue pencil upon the margin. It seemed dull and dead about the lobby and also in the streets. The hotel manager said the Casino, an adjoining hall, was at our service, free, and the keeper had instructions to seat and light it. Dinner time came

and we all went down together. It was Mark's first appearance in a public dining room since we started. He attracted some attention as he entered and sat down, but nothing especial transpired. After dinner the news stand man told me he had not sold a ticket, and no one had enquired about them. I waited until eight o'clock and went to the hall to notify the man that he need not light up, as there would be no audience. The janitor and I stood chatting until about half past eight. I was about to leave when a man and woman came to the door and asked for tickets. I was about to tell them there would be no lecture when I saw a number of people, guests of the house, coming. So I suddenly changed my mind and told them: "Admission $1.00. Pay the money to me and walk right in." The crowd kept rushing on me and I was obliged to ask everybody who could to please have the exact amount ready, as I was unable to change large bills without a good deal of delay. It was after nine o'clock before the rush was over and I sent a boy for "Mark." He expressed his pleasant surprise. I asked him to walk to the platform and introduce himself, which he did. I don't believe there was ever an audience that had a better time of an hour and a half. Mark was simply immense.

I counted my money while the show was going on and found I had taken in $398. When the entertainment was about half over, two young men came to the door and wanted to be admitted for $1.00 for the two. I said, "No, $1.00 each. I cannot take less." They turned to go, when I called them back and explained that I needed two more dollars to make receipts just $400., and said: "Now, if you'll pay a dollar each and complete my pile, you can come in and enjoy the best end of the programme, and when the show is out I'll take you down stairs and blow you off to twice that amount." They paid the two dollars and after the crowd had left the hall, I introduced them to Mark and we all went down to the billiard room, had a good time until 12 o'clock, and Mark and I made two delightful acquaintances. This has been one of our best days. Mark is gaining.

Saturday, July 20th, Mackinac to Petoskey.

"Mark" and I left the ladies at The Grand and went to Petoskey on the two o'clock train and boat. The smoke is so thick as to be almost stifling. There are forest fires on both sides of the track. There is a good hotel here. Mark dressed his carbuncle himself without assistance. He is surely gaining. We had a full house, and for the first time in a number of years I had a lecture room so crowded at $1.00 a ticket that many could not get standing room and were obliged to go away. The theatre has a seating capacity of five hundred, but over seven hundred and fifty got in. "Mark's" programme was just right—one hour and twenty minutes. He stopped at an hour and ten minutes, and cries of "Go on! Go on!" were so earnest that he told one more story. George Kennan was one of the audience. He is going to give a course of lectures at Lake View Assembly, an auxiliary Chautauqua adjoining Petoskey, where about five thousand people assemble every summer. Mr. Hall, the manager, thought that "Mark Twain" would not draw sufficient to warrant engaging him, so I took the risk outside, and won.

Sunday, July 21st.

"Mark" and I left Petoskey for Mackinac at 5:30 this morning, to spend Sunday. It was severe on the poor man, but he was heroic and silent all the way. He has not tasted food since the dinner on the Faxton, Friday.

Monday, July 22nd.

On Lake Superior. S. S. Northwest. We went on deck early and found the smoke all gone and the sun shining brightly, but it has been so cold all day that few passengers are on deck. It took us a long time to pass through the Locks, although our big steamer had the right of way and Capt. Brown and Purser Pierce did all they could to hurry us on, for we were already eight hours late. There are hundreds of sailing and steam craft waiting their turn to pass through. The lock's capacity is tested every moment from the opening to the closing of navigation. I counted upwards of six hundred craft during the day yesterday. The commerce of these lakes is astonishingly great, and little known by the eastern people.

We landed at Duluth at just 9 P.M. Mr. Briggs, our correspondent, met us at the wharf with a carriage. As our boat neared land, Briggs shouted:

"Hello, Major Pond."

"Hello, Briggs".

"Is Mark Twain all right?"

"Yes, he is ready to go to the hall. He will be the first passenger off the ship".

"Good. We have a big audience waiting for him", said Mr. Briggs.

"We'll have them convulsed in ten minutes", said I.

"Mark" was the first passenger to land. Mr. Briggs hurried him to the church, which was packed with twelve hundred and fifty warm friends (100° in the shade) to meet and greet him. It was a big audience. Got through at 10:50. Were all on board train for Minneapolis at 11:20. <Gross: $902.00.>

It was my busy night. The train for Minneapolis was to start at 12 o'clock. The agents in New York who had fitted me out with transportation and promised that everything should be in readiness on our arrival in Duluth, had forgotten us, and no arrangements for sleeper or transfer of baggage had been made. I had all this to attend to, besides looking after the business part of the lecture, which was on sharing terms with a church society. Everything mixed up, as the door–tender and finance committee were bound to hear the lecture. I could get no statement, but took all the money in sight, and "Mark" and I got on board the train as it was starting for Minneapolis[.]

Tuesday, July 23.

Minneapolis 7:30. West Hotel,–a delightful place. Six skilled reporters spent about two hours with Mark. He was lying in bed, and very tired, I know, but he was extremely courteous to them and they all enjoyed the interview. The Metropolitan Opera House was filled to the top gallery with a big crowd of well-dressed, intelligent people. It was about as big a night as Mark ever had, to my knowledge. He had a new entertainment, blending pathos with humor, with unusual continuity. This was at Mrs. Clemens' suggestion. She had given me an idea on the start that too much humor tired an audience with laughing. Mark took the hint and worked in three or four pathetic stories that make the entertainment perfect. The "show" is a triumph, and Mark will never need a running mate to make him satisfactory to everybody.

The next day the Minneapolis papers were full of good things about the lecture. "The Times" devoted three columns and a half of fine print to a verbatim report of it. The following evening in St. Paul, Mark gave the same programme, which was commented on in glowing terms by St. Paul papers.

Thursday, July 25, 1900 [1895].

Mr. Chute, who had had the Minneapolis lectures, sent baskets of flowers to the ladies, and Mrs. Clemens invited him to dine with us. Mark was not very attentive to him, and after dinner Mrs. Clemens reminded him of his seeming impoliteness, whereupon Mark wrote Mr. Chute a letter of thanks, regret and praise, such as few people ever received from that source. Mr. Chute proudly showed it to me and said he would rather have that letter than $1,000. profit on the lecture.

Friday, July 26th.

Winnipeg. The Manitoba. We have had a most charming ride through North Dakota and South-east Manitoba. It seems as if everything along the route must have been put in order for our reception. The flat wild prairies (uninhabited in 1883) are now all under cultivation. There are fine farm houses, barns, wind mills and vast fields of wheat—"oceans of wheat" as Mark said—as far as the eye can reach in all directions, stirred into billows by the wind like the waves of the sea, and all the country so flat! Mr. Beecher remarked to his wife when riding through here in '83: "Mother, you couldn't flatter this country."

We had a splendid audience. Mark and I were entertained at the Manitoba Club after the lecture—a club of the leading men of Winnipeg. We did not stay out very late as Mark feared Mrs. Clemens would not retire until he came, and he was quite anxious for her to rest, as the long night journey in the cars had been very fatiguing. On our arrival at the hotel we heard singing and a sound of revelry in the parlors. A party of young gentlemen of the reception committee had escorted our ladies home. They were fine singers, and, with Clara at the piano, a concert was in progress that we all enjoyed for another hour.

Saturday, July 27th.

We all put down this day as the pleasantest we have thus far spent. Several young English gentlemen who have staked fortunes in this northwest, in wheat ranches and other prime enterprises, brought out their tandems and traps and drove the ladies about the country. They saw the largest herd of wild buffalo that now exists, in a large enclosure. They were also shown the various interesting suburban sights, of which there are more than one would believe could exist in this far northwestern city. Bouquets and banks of flowers of most beautiful colors were sent in. Many ladies called, and all in all it has been an ovation. Mark, as is his custom, did not get up until it was time to go to the lecture hall, but he was happy. Several journalists called whom he told me were the best informed and the most scholarly lot of newspaper men he had found anywhere, and I believe he was correct. There was another large crowd at the lecture, and another and final reception at the famous Manitoba Club. We were back at the hotel at twelve, and all so happy! We are surely on the real road to true happiness.

Sunday, July 28, 1895.

We arrived in Crookston on the christening night of the new hotel. Mark Twain's name was the first on its register. We did not get there until after dark and had to remain in darkness a couple of hours until the electrician could get the incandescent lights adjusted in our room. But Mark was in bed ten minutes after our arrival and did not get up until time for the lecture next day. We have travelled all day through an ocean of wheat.

Monday, July 29th.

We have been at Crookston, Minn., all day. We have been the first and especially favored guests of this fine new hotel, "The Crookston". "Mark Twain's" name was the first on the register. We are enjoying it. Mark is as gay as a lark, but he remained in bed until time to go to the Opera House. This city is wonderfully improved since I was here in '83 with Mr. Beecher, and in '85 with Clara Louise Kellogg, and in '87 with Charles

Dickens, 2nd. The opening of this house is a great event. People are filling up the town from all directions to see and hear "Mark", and taking advantage of the occasion to see the first new hotel in their vicinity with hot and cold water, electric lights, and all modern improvements.

Tuesday, July 30, 1895.

This morning we had our first experience of being obliged to get out at the unseasonable hour of 3:30 in the morning to take the four o'clock overland train from Crookston, but it has done us all good. Even Clara enjoyed the unique experience. It refreshed her memory. She recollected that she had telegraphed to Elmira to have her winter cloak expressed to Crookston. Fortunately the express agent was sleeping in his office near the station. We disturbed his slumbers to find the great cloak, which was another acquisition to our sixteen pieces of hand baggage. There were five in our party: Mr. and Mrs. Clemens and their daughter Clara; Mrs. Pond and myself. We were all at the depot five minutes before the train was due, only to read on the bulletin board: "Pacific Mail one hour and twenty minutes late." It was a chilly morning, and the passenger room with its rough benches very dreary, so we all paced up and down the platform waiting. Mark began to grumble and we all thought him unreasonably cross. He had contracted with Pond to travel, he said, and to give entertainments, and not to stand shivering around depots at this inhuman hour waiting for delayed trains that never were known to arrive. He kept this up for some time, much to my discomfort, when finally Mrs. Clemens, whose influence is always instantaneous, asked him if he was not a little unreasonable. He was standing at the time by the baggage truck on which he sat down, at the same time answering his wife, "No, I am not unreasonable. I insist on Pond keeping his contract to the letter by travelling me on this truck." So I wheeled him about the station just as the five o'clock sun was coming up, and Clara got a snap shot of the act, which Mark said would be documentary evidence of my having keep the agreement.

When we boarded the train, we found five lower berths (which means five sections) ready for us; a splendid dining car, à la carte, and excellent cooking. The level prairies of North Dakota wheat just turning, and the whole country a lovely green, all the afternoon; and then the arid plains, the cactus, Buffalo grass, jack rabbits, and wild life, and the Missouri River, dear old friend that had bourn both of us on her muddy bosom many a <day> time. It was a great day for "Mark", and also for me. The ladies were enthusiastic in proportion, to see that "Mark" and I were boys again, travelling our native heath.

Wednesday, July 31st.

Great Falls, Montana,—Park Hotel. Arrived here at 7:30 after a good night's sleep. The interest grows more and more intense as we come near to the Rocky Mountains. It brings back fond memories of other days. Two Brothers Gibson, proprietors of the hotel, drove our party out to Giant Spring, three miles. It is a giant, too. I never saw a more beautiful or wonderful spring. A river fairly boils up out of the ground and the most beautiful deep peacock green color I ever saw in clear water. <No one here that knows about the business. No notices in the papers; no one seems to know or care about our coming. The first time there has been no advance sale. Receipts of evening were only $220.50. We get 70% of that.> The largest copper ore smelters in the world are here. The Great Falls are water power enough for all the machinery west of Chicago, with some to spare.

"Mark" is improving. For the first time since we started he appeared about the hotel corridors and on the street. He and I walked about the outskirts of the town, and I caught a number of interesting snap shots among the Norwegian shanties. I got a good group including four generations, with eight children, a calf, and five cats. "Mark" wanted a photograph of each cat. He caught a pair of kittens in his arms, greatly to the discomfort of their owner, a little girl. He tried to make friends with the child, and buy the kitties, but she began to cry and beg that her pets might be liberated. He soon captured her with a pretty story, and finally consented to let them go. Few know "Mark's" great love for cats, as well as for every living creature.

Thursday, August 1st.

Great Falls to Butte, Montana. Started at 7:35. All seem tired. The light air and the long drive yesterday told very much on <Mark> us all.

Mark had an off night and was not at his best, which has almost broken his heart. He couldn't get over it all day. The Gibson Brothers have done much to make our visit delightful, and it has proved very enjoyable indeed. Of course being proprietors of the hotel they lose nothing, for I find they charge us $5.00 a day each, and the extortions from porters, baggage–men, and bell-boys, surpass anything I ever heard of. The smallest money is two bits here—absurd.

Aug. 2.

Butte, Mont. We enter the Rocky Mountains through a cañon of the Upper Missouri. We have climbed mountains all day, and at Butte are nearly 8.000 feet high. It tells on me, but the others escape. Mrs. Clemens says it has been one of the most interesting days of her life. "Mark" has taken great interest in everything, but kept from talking. <On our arrival in Butte he went directly to bed, and did not get up> After reaching the hotel he kept quiet in bed until he went to the hall. He more than made up for last night's disappointment. He was at his best. I escorted Mrs. Clemens and Clara to a box in the theatre, expecting to return immediately to the hotel, but I found myself listening and sat through the lecture enjoying every word. <Never have I> It actually seemed as if I had never known him quite so good. He was great. The house was full and very responsive.

After the lecture many of his former Nevada friends came forward to greet him. We went to a fine Club, where champagne and stories blended until twelve, much to the delight of many gentlemen. Mark never drinks champagne. His is hot Scotch winter and summer, without any sugar, and never before 11 p.m.

Friday, August 2nd.

Butte to Anaconda with "Mark" without the ladies. We left the hotel at 4:30 by trolley car in order to have plenty of time to reach the train. We had gone only three blocks, when the power gave out and we could not move. It was twelve minutes to five. No carriage in sight. We tried to get a grocery wagon but the mean owner refused to take us for less than $10.00. I told him to go to ---. I saw another grocery wagon near by, and told its owner I would pay any price to reach that train. "Mark" and I mounted the seat with him. He laid the lash on his pair of broncos, and I think quicker time was never made to that depot. We reached the train just as the conductor had shouted "All Aboard" and signalled the engineer. The train was moving as we jumped on. The driver charged me a dollar, but I handed him two.

At Anaconda we found a very fine hotel and several friends very anxiously waiting to meet "Mark." Elaborate arrangements had been made to lunch him and give him a lively day among his old mountain friends, as he had been expected by the morning train. Fortunately, he missed this demonstration and was in good condition for the evening. He was introduced by the mayor of the city in a witty address of welcome. Here was our first small audience, where the local manager came out a trifle the loser.

A little incident connected with our experience here shows "Mark Twain's" generosity. The local manager was a man who had known "Mark" in the sixties, and was very anxious to secure him for a lecture in Anaconda. He therefore contracted to pay the price asked, [<deleted sum>]. Anaconda is a small city, whose chief industry is a large smelting foundry. There were not enough people interested in high class entertainments to make up a paying audience, and the manager was short about $60. I took what he had, and *all* he had, giving him a receipt in full. As "Mark" and I were not equal partners, of course the larger share of the loss fell to him. I explained the circumstances when we had our next settlement at the end of the week, hoping for his approval.

"And you took the last cent that poor fellow had! Send him a hundred dollars, and if you can't afford to stand your share, charge it all to me. I'm not going around robbing poor men who are disappointed in their calculations as to my commercial value. I'm poor, and working to pay debts that I never contracted, but I don't want to get money in that way".

I sent the money, and was glad to have the honor of standing my share. The letter of acknowledgment from that man brought out the following expression from "Mark": "I wish that every hundred dollars I ever invested had produced the same amount of happiness["].

In Helena (August 3) the people did not care for lectures. They all liked "Mark", and enjoyed meeting him, but there was no public enthusiasm for the man that has made the early history of that mining country romantic and famous all over the world. The Montana Club entertained him grandly after the lecture, and he met many old friends and acquaintances. Some of them had come all the way from Virginia City, to see their former comrade of the mining camps.

One man, now very rich, came from Virginia City, Nevada, on purpose to see Mark and settle an old score. When the glasses were filled and Mark's health proposed, this man interrupted the proceedings by saying:

"Hold on a minute. Before we go further I want to say to you, Sam Clemens, that you did me a dirty trick over there in Silver City, and I've come here to have a settlement with you."

Deathly silence prevailed for a moment, when Mark said, in his deliberate drawl:

"Let's see. That – was – before – I – reformed, – wasn't – it?"

Senator Sanders suggested that inasmuch as the other fellow had never reformed, Clemens and all the others present should forgive him and drink together, which all did. Thus the row was broken up before it commenced and all was well. Mark told stories until after twelve. We walked from the Club back to the hotel up quite a mountain—the first hard walk Mark has had. He stands the light air and is getting strong.

Helena, Sunday, August 4th.

We all slept late. The dry burning sun makes life almost intolerable. There has been scarcely a soul on the streets all day. "Mark" and I had a good time at the Montana Club last night. He simply beats the world telling stories, but we find some bright lights here. There were present Senator Sanders, Hon. Major Maginnus, Hon. Hugh McQuade, Mr. A. J. Seligman, Judge Knowles, of the U.S. Supreme Court, who introduced Mr. Beecher in Deer Lodge and Butte in '83, Mr. L. A. Walker, Dr. C. K. Cole, A. J. Steele and Mr. Frank L. Sizer. We have very heavy mails, but we are all too tired to open and read any letters that are not absolutely necessary.

Mark lay around all day in his room on the floor, reading and writing in his note book, and smoking. In the gloaming Dr. Cole, with his trotters, drove Mark and Mrs. Clemens out to Broadwater, four miles. The heat gave way to a delicious balmy breeze that invigorated everybody. How delightful these summer evenings in the Rocky Mountains.

Missoula, Mont., August 5th.

Senator Sanders and Mark walked to the station in Helena this morning, while I accompanied the ladies in a carriage. Who should we meet walking on the station platform but Mrs. Henry Ward Beecher, on her way to visit her son Herbert, in Port Townsend. It was a delightful surprise. Senator Sanders at once recognized her, as in 1883, with her husband, he joined our party and drove from Helena, then the end of the eastern section of the Northern Pacific R.R., to Missoula, the eastern end of the western section. We then drove in a carriage with four horses, via Butte and Deer Lodge. It took four days to make the journey. Senator Sanders traveled with us to-day the same distance, in five hours, in a Pullman car. At Missoula we all drove in a bus to the Florence Hotel, the ladies inside and Mark and I outside with the driver. Here we saw the first sign of the decadence of the horse: a man riding a bicycle along side of the bus, leading a horse to a nearby blacksmith shop. At "Mark's" suggestion I caught a snap shot of the scene.

Officers from Fort Missoula, four miles out, had driven in with an ambulance and an invitation from Lieut. Col. Burt, Commandant, for our entire party to drive out to the Fort. The ladies accepted. Mark went to bed and I looked after the business. We had a large audience in a small hall. The patrons were mainly officers of the Fort and their families, and it was a gathering of people that appreciated the occasion. Many of the ladies who marry officers are from our best eastern society. After the lecture the meeting took the form of a social reception and it was midnight before it broke up.

As we do not leave until 2:30 to-morrow, we have all accepted an invitation to witness guard mounting and to lunch early at the Fort.

August 6th.

Two army ambulances were sent to the hotel for our party and Adjutant Gen. Ruggles, who is here in a tour of inspection. "Mark" rose early and said he would walk to the Fort slowly; he thought it would do him good. Gen. Ruggles and the ladies went in one ambulance (the old four-mule army officer's ambulance) and the other waited some little time before starting, that I might complete arrangements for all the party to go direct from the Fort to the depot. I was the only passenger in it, riding with the driver and enjoying former like experiences on the plains when in the army. We were about half way to the Fort when I discovered a man walking hurriedly toward us, quite a distance away to our left. I was sure it was "Mark" and asked the driver to slow up. In a minute I saw him signal to us, and I asked the driver to turn and drive towards him. We were on a level plain, and through that clear mountain atmosphere one can see a <long> great distance. We were not long in reaching our man, much to his relief. He had come out alone and taken the wrong road, and did not discover his mistake until he had walked five or six miles on it. He was countermarching when he saw our ambulance and ran across to meet us. He *was* tired— too tired to express disgust—and sat quietly inside the ambulance until we drove up to headquarters, where were a number of officers and ladies, besides our party. As "Mark" stepped out, a colored sergeant laid hands on him, saying:

"Are you Mark Twain?"

"I am."

"I have orders to arrest <you> and take you to the guard house."

"All right."

And the sergeant marched him across the parade ground to the guard house, he not uttering a word of protest.

Immediately followed Lieut. Col. Burt and the ambulance hurried over, to relieve the prisoner. Col Burt very fervently asked Mark's pardon for the practical joke and asked him to ride back to headquarters. Mark said, "Thanks, I prefer freedom if you don't mind. I'll walk. I see you have thorough discipline here," casting an approving eye to[ward] the sargeant who had had him under arrest.

The garrison was 7 companies of the 27th U.S. Colored Regiment. A military band of 30 pieces. Guard mount was delayed for Gen. Ruggles and our inspection. <Then luncheon.> The band played quite a programme, and we all declared it one of the finest military bands in America. We witness[ed] some fine drilling of the soldiers, and we learned that for this kind of service the colored soldiers were more subordinate, and submissive to rigid drill and discipline than white men, and <that there were> seldom desertions.

<As we started from the Missoula Station> Attached to our train from Missoula Station were two special cars, bearing an excursion party of the new Reciever of the Northern Pacific Railroad, and his friends, one of whom was the U. S. Supreme Judge who had appointed this reciever. An invitation was sent in to Mark to ride in their car, but as it only came for him alone and not the ladies he declined. It was an enjoyable ride to Spokane, where we arrived at 11:30—*Spokane House*, the largest hotel I ever saw. A large commercial <block> building covering an entire block or mor[e] revamped into a hotel. A whole store diverted into one bed room and nicely furnished too. Reporters in waiting to interview the distinguished guest. Mark is gaining in strength and is enjoying everything, and the interviewers had [a] good time.

All day August 8 in Spokane. Hotel full. The new Reciever and his gay party are spending the day, but all leave just before time for the lecture.

In the forenoon Mark and I walked about this remarkable city, with its asphalt streets, electric lights, nine story telegraph poles, and commercial blocks that would do credit to any Eastern city. Buildings ten stories high, with the nine top stories empty. Many fine stores with great plate glass fronts "*to rent*." Afternoon we drove about the city, our entire party in an open carriage. Our driver pointed out some beautiful suburban residences, and told us who occupied them. "That house," said he, as we drove by a palatial establishment, "is where Mr Brown lives. He is receiver for the Spook Bank, which failed last year for over $2,000,000. You all know about that big failure, of course. The Receiver lives there."

Another, "That man, living up in that big house is receiver for the Great Falls Company. It failed for nearly a million. The President and directors of that Company are most all in the State Prison, and this 'yere house that we are coming to now is where the Receiver of the Wash. Gas & Water Company lives," &c.

Mark said to the ladies, "If I had a son to send West I would educate him for a receiver. It seems to be about the only thriving industry." We find here a magnificent new theater—*The Opera House*. It has cost over $200,000, and never yet was a quarter filled. The manager was awfully disappointed at reciepts of the lecture. He had counted on a full house. Where he expected the people to come from I never could imagine. The reciepts were not much better than Missoula. Mark didn't enjoy it—and manifested no delicacy in so expressing himself.

The gross receipts were only $262., in spirt of the fact that The Daily Times, "the official daily of Spokane County" warned its readers that "those who fail to attend his lecture to-night, will miss one of the rarest treats of their lives". My opinion is that the local manager was not energetic.

As we have a day here the ladies have overhauled and re-packed their trunks. I think there is no occupation that has the fascination for women when traveling as the unpacking and overhauling large traveling trunks. They go at it early and miss their luncheon and are late to dinner and show no signs of fatigue. There are two ladies that I would like to pit against each other in an international <match> trunk–packing tournament. Mrs. Clemens and Mrs. Dr. Watson (Ian Maclaren) [.] I would give Mrs Clemens four large Saratoga trunks to manipulate and Mrs. Watson two large English portmanteaus and seven small bags including soiled linen bag and a few catch all's. Mrs C. to stand on her feet with her back bent <over> to her work and Mrs. W. not rise from her knees during the performance. This business seems to enhance the power of endurance for delicate women, as nothing else can.

Another incident here. Our ladies dressed their best for dinner and outshone the recievers' excursionists who occupied most of the great dining hall. Mark didn't see it as he never comes down to dinner. I know I saw it and I enjoyed a feeling of <envy> pride. I just felt and knew I was envied by the men at the other tables. Clar[a] Clemens is the most beautiful girl I ever saw. As we passed out of the dining room into [the] great parlor she sat down to the large Chickering grand piano, and began playing a Chopin nocturne. It was in the gloaming. Stealthily guests from the dining room came in and sat breathlessly in remote parts of the boundless room listening to a performance that would do credit to any great pianist. Never did I witness a more beautiful sight than this sweet brunett unconsciously holding a large audience of charmed listeners. Her mother saw and heard her and if it was not one of the <happiest> supreme moments of her life, then I have guessed wrong. It was an incident forever fixed in my memory.

That night at 11:30 we went aboard the Sleepers on the Great Northern Road. Everything was in readiness for us. The next day was one full of interest as we ride over the Rockies on the zigzag road, traveling over 30 miles to make seven. Mark rode on the engine[,] greatly to the delight of the engineer.

We transferred at Seattle, to the little "Grey Hound of Puget Sound"—*The Flyer*—said to be the fastest steamer in the world. Mark sat on the deck of the Flyer watching its baggage-smashers removing our trunks from the baggage car to the truck which was to convey them to the Flyer, at Seattle[.] [H]e exclaimed, "Oh! how I do wish one of those trunks were filled with dynamite and that all the baggage–destroyers on earth were gathered about it, and I just far enough off to see them hurled into Kingdom Come!"

We arrived in Tacoma at 5 o'clock and have sumptuous apartments at The Tacoma—a gem caravansary built by the Northern Pacific R. R. Co. The receiver is an old friend of mine, formerly a contractor on the N. P. R. R. Another friend also, C. J. T. [?] Prescott[,] one of the prosperous. He is local receiver of the Northern Pacific R. R., the highest distinction a man can attain out here. This is another overgrown metropolis. We can't see it nor anything else owing to the dense smoke everywhere.

Here in Tacoma the ladies are to remain and rest while "Mark" and I "take in" Portland and Olympia.

Thursday, August 8th. [repeated material]

Tacoma, Wash.—The Tacoma. Arrived at five o'clock. Never has a country so changed. This is another overgrown metropolis. We can't see it, nor anything else, owing to the dense smoke everywhere. At Seattle we waited an hour and a half, and I had to change transportation. We are in danger of being late at Portland and may be obliged to charter a train. Our ride by a pretty little steamer, the Flyer, from Seattle to Tacoma, was intensely interesting.

"Mark" is at his best in vituperative adjectives this morning. He will "never travel in America again". Every comfort possible on the journey, but he is not travelling for comfort; he is travelling and lecturing to pay debts that somebody else contracted. Watching the baggage-smashers removing our trunks from the baggage car to the truck which was to convey them to the Flyer, he exclaimed, "Oh, how I do wish one of those trunks were filled with dynamite and that all the baggage-destroyers on earth were gathered about it, and I just far enough off to see them hurled into Kingdom Come!"

Friday, August 9th.

Portland, Oregon, (from Tacoma). Left at 2:35 P.M., train forty minutes late, but we made up the time, the conductor and engineer having been instructed to make it. Mr. S. E. Moffett, of the *San Francisco Examiner* appeared. He is "Mark's" nephew and resembles his uncle very much. On his arrival, "Mark" took occasion to blaspheme for a few minutes that his relatives might realize that men are not all alike. He cursed the journey, the fatigues and annoyances, winding up by acknowledging that if everything had been made and arranged by the Almighty for the occasion, it could not have been better or more comfortable, but he "was not traveling for pleasure," etc.

Mark Twain's Cigar Case
Made of "The Skin of a Young Lady."

While on the train going from Tacoma to Portland, Mark and I made the acquaintance of a Mr. Geo. M. Paschall, whose father had been editor of the "Missouri Republican" during the days of Mark's life on the Mississippi River, and a Mr. Ames, a young lawyer and graduate of Yale. We were in the smoking compartment and Mark offered these gentlemen cigars from his full cigar case, which he remarked to them was made from the skin of a lady, and he related the following story.

"While I was traveling in Europe I visited Prof. Flammarion, the greatest French astronomer, in company with Prof. Holden, of the Lick Observatory in California. You ought to have heard the conversation between those two scientific men. It was an intellectual tournament and I was the only auditor. To my enthusiastic expressions of envy of the Professor for his great knowledge and the delight his conversation had given me, he replied that my appreciation reminded him of a late lady friend, who was so earnest in her declarations of the delight his books and lectures had given her that she said:

" 'Professor, I do wish there was something that I might do to show my appreciation, in return for all the pleasure you have given me.'

"She was a beautiful woman, with the fairest complexion and the most beautiful shoulders and neck I ever saw. I said to her:

" 'I think if I had your beautiful neck and shoulders and complexion I would be perfectly satisfied. I would aspire to nothing higher than to own them.'

"She replied: 'Well, when I am through with them I will send them to you.' She died a few years later, and to my surprise I found that she had left directions that the skin of her neck and shoulders be sent to me, and, pointing to a beautifully bound volume on his centre table, this book is bound with that lady's skin."

"The lady," continued Mark, "of whose skin my cigar case was made probably had the small pox very bad." (It was an alligator skin case.)

He and I reached Portland on time, 8:22, and found the Marquam Grand packed with a waiting audience, and the sign "Standing Room Only" out. It was a grand success. <Gross $800.> After the lecture Mark's friend Col. Wood, formerly of the U. S. Army, gave a supper at the Portland Club where the about two dozen of the leading men were entertained with for two hours with Mark's story telling. They will all remember that evening as long as they live. There is surely but one Mark Twain.

Saturday, August 10th.

Portland to Olympia. Smoke, smoke, smoke. It was not easy to tear ourselves away from Portland so early. *The Oregonian* contains one of the best notices that "Mark" has had. He is pleased with it and is very jolly today.

We left for Olympia at eleven o'clock, via N.P.R.R. Somehow, "Mark" seems to grow greater from day to day. Each time it seemed as though his entertainment had reached perfection, but last night surpassed all. A gentleman on the train, a physician, from Portland, said that no man ever left a better impression on a Portland audience; that "Mark Twain" was the theme on the streets, and in all business places. A young reporter for *The Oregonian* met "Mark" as he was boarding the train for Olympia. Probably five minutes talk. He wrote a two column interview, which "Mark" declared was the most accurate and the best that had ever been reported of him.

On the train a bevy of young ladies ventured to introduce themselves to him, and he entertained them all the way to Olympia, where a delegation of leading citizens met us, headed by John Miller Murphy, editor of the oldest paper in Washington. We were met outside of the city, in order that we might enjoy a ride on a new trolley car to the town. As "Mark" stepped from the train, Mr. Miller said: "Mr. Twain, as chairman of the reception committee, allow me to welcome you to the capital of the youngest and most picturesque state in the Union. I am sorry the smoke is so dense that you cannot see our mountains and our forests, which are now on fire". "Mark" said, "I regret to see—I mean to learn (I can't see, of course, for the smoke) that your magnificent forests are being destroyed by fire. As for the smoke, I do not so much mind. I am accustomed to that. I am a perpetual smoker myself".

Sunday, August 11, 1895.

We are at the Olympia, a very pleasant hotel, made to accommodate large gatherings when the legislature meets every other yr. On this occasion Mark and I and 2 traveling men, — the only guests. The hotel clerk performs the function of waiter—and a very polite and considerate waiter he was—also bartender, porter and bell boy.

Mark had his breakfast in his room and declared that it was nice to have a quiet breakfast and not be interrupted. (See picture.)

Monday, August 12th.

Tacoma, Wash. The Tacoma. Had trouble in settling at the Opera House. <Heilig> The manager is a scamp. Expected trouble and had it. <Heilig is trying to avoid his contract and construe it as meaning that we were guaranteed $500. on the two lectures in Portland and Tacoma, not $250. guarantee on each night with 60% gross. He uses my letter, which did read to that effect, but which was written long before the contract was signed.>

The Tacoma Press Club gave "Mark" a reception after the lecture in their rooms. It was a very bright affair. "Mark" is finding out that he has found his friends by the loss of his fortune. People are constantly meeting him on the street, and at halls, and in hotels, telling him of the happiness he has brought them,—old and young alike. He seems as fresh to the rising

generation as he is dear to older friends. Here we met Lieut. Commander Wadhams, who is executive officer of the "Mohican", now in Seattle Harbor. He has invited us all on board the man-of-war to dine to-morrow. And we have all accepted.

Great audience in Seattle the next <day> evening. <we had a fine business.> "Standing room only" again. <Gross [illegible figure.]> "Mark" was hoarse, but the hoarseness seemed to augment the volume of his voice.

He met many of his friends and admirers at the Ranier Club after the lecture. Surely he is finding out that his misfortunes are his blessings. He has been the means of more real pleasure to his readers and hearers than he ever could have imagined had not this opportunity presented itself.

Wednesday, August 14th.

Seattle to Whatcom. "Mark's" cold is getting worse. He worried and fretted all day. He had only two swearing fits; with but a short interval between them they lasted from our arrival in town until he went to sleep after midnight. It was with great difficulty he got through the lecture. The crowd, stringing in from long distances and at long intervals until after half past nine, made him so nervous that he left the stage for a time. I thought he was ill and rushed to the stage, only to meet him in a white rage. He looked daggers at me, and remarked:

"You'll never play a trick like this on me again. Look at that d--- audience. It isn't half in yet". I replied that the cars ran only every half hour, and that was why the last installment came so late. He cooled down and went at it again. He captured the crowd. Had a good time and an encore and was obliged to give an additional story.

Thursday, August 15th.

Vancouver, B. C., The Vancouver. "Mark's" throat is in a very bad condition. It was a great effort to make himself heard. <Mrs. Clemens and I both suffered for the poor man.> He is a thoroughbred. A great man,—with wonderful will power, or he would have succumbed. We had a <good> fine audience, house crowded, very English, and I think "Mark" liked it. Everything here is English and Canadian. There is a rumor afloat that the country about is beautiful. We can't see it. Smoke, smoke, everywhere, and no relief. My eyes are sore from it. We are told that the "War[r]imoo" will not sail until Wednesday, so I have arranged for the Victoria lecture Tuesday.

Friday, August 16th.

Vancouver. Our tour across the continent is virtually finished and I feel the reaction. "Othello's occupation gone". "Mark" had a doctor this morning who says he is not seriously ill. Mrs. Clemens is curing him. The more I see of this lady, the greater and more wonderful she appears to be. There are few women that could manage and absolutely rule such a nature as "Mark's". She knows the gentle and smooth way over every obstruction he meets, and makes everything lovely. This has indeed been the most delightful tour I have ever made with any party, and I wish to record it as one of the most enjoyable of all my managerial experiences. I hardly ever expect another. "Mark" has written in a presentation copy of "Roughing It":

> "Here ends one of the smoothest and pleasantest trips across
> the continent that any group of five has ever made".

"Mark" is better this evening and we surely shall have a good lecture in Victoria.

Saturday, August 17th.

Vancouver. We are all waiting for the news as to when the "Warrimoo" will be off the dry dock and ready to sail. "Mark" is getting better. Have booked Victoria for Tuesday the 20th, <and then May and I go to Port Townsend, Seattle, and home.>

Mark in bed as usual. Reporters are anxious to meet and interview him, and I have urged it. He finally said, "If they'll excuse my bed, show them up." They came up, a quartet of bright young English *journalists*. They all had a good time and made much of "the last interview with Mark Twain in America"—and so it was.

"Mark" has lain in bed all day. He is writing <somewhat but very nervous.>, and in excellent spirits. His throat is better.

Vancouver, Sunday, August 18, 1895.

We have finally had an escapade. Mrs. Chase and her son, who heard me lecture at Chautauqua, wanted me to give a little entertainment in the parlors. Mrs. Clemens wanted me to do so, too. So did Clara, but after all arrangements had been completed, "Mark" would not allow it, on the ground that I was still his manager, so everything had to be stopped. It threw a wet blanket on all of us.

Monday, August 19th.

Vancouver still, and smoke is as firmly fixed as the town. It is bad. "Mark" has <been feeble all day.> not been very cheerful to-day. He doesn't get his voice back. <He is weak, and seems to have collapsed.> He and I took a walk about the streets and he seemed <to[o] weak to walk.> discouraged. I think on account of Mrs. Clemens' dread of the long voyage and the unfavorable stories of the Warrimoo.

Slight rain to-day, but the smoke is more <powerful> dense than ever. We leave Vancouver and hosts of new friends for Victoria, B.C., and then we part. That is not easy, for we are all very happy. It does make my heart ache to see "Mark" so <weak> downhearted after such continued success as he has had.

On August 20th the boat for Victoria arrived half an hour late. We all hurried to get on board, only to be told by the Captain that he had 180 tons of freight to discharge, and that it would be four o'clock before we left. This lost our Victoria engagement, and I was obliged to telegraph and postpone it.

Mark was not in condition to relish this news, and as he stood on the wharf, after the ladies had gone aboard, he took occasion to tell the Captain [in] very loud and unpious language his opinion of a passenger carrying company that for a few dollars extra would violate their contract and obligations to the public. They were a lot of --- somethings, and deserved the penitentiary. The Captain listened without response, but got very red in the face. It seems that the ladies had overheard the loud talk. Soon after Mark joined them he came to me and asked if I wouldn't see that Captain and apologize for his unmanly abuse and see if any possible restitution could be made. I did and the Captain and Mark became <great> quite friends.

We left Vancouver on The Charmer at six o'clock, arriving in Victoria a little after midnight.

Wednesday, August 21st.

Victoria, B.C. The Driad. "Mark" has been in bed all day. He doesn't seem to get strength. He smokes constantly, and I fear it is too much, still he may stand it. Physicians say it will eventually kill him.

We had a good audience. Lord and Lady Aberdeen in a box, who came back on the stage after the lecture and said many very nice things of the entertainment, offering to write to friends in Australia about it. Mark's voice began strong but showed fatigue towards the last. His audience[,] one of the most appreciative he ever had[,] was in great sympathy with him as they realized <his condition> the effort he was obliged to make, owing to his hoarseness.

A telegram from Mr. George McL. Brown says the "War[r]imoo" will sail at six o'clock to–morrow evening. This is the last appearance of "Mark Twain" in America for more than a year, I know, and I much fear the very last, for it doesn't seem possible that his physical strength can hold out. After the lecture to–night he expected to visit a club with Mr. Campbell, who did not come round. He and I went out for a walk. He was tired and feeble. He did not want to come back to the hotel. He was nervous, and weak, and disappointed. He had expected to entertain and meet a lot of gentlemen. He and I are alike in one respect,—we don't relish disappointment.

Thursday, August 21st [22nd].

Victoria yet. The blessed "tie that binds" seems to be drawing tighter and tighter as the time for our final separation approaches. We shall never be happier in any combination, and Mrs. Clemens is the great magnet. What a noble woman she is! It is Mark Twain's wife who makes his works so <popular> great. She edits everything and brings purity, dignity, and sweetness to his writings. In "Joan of Arc" I see Mrs. Clemens as much as "Mark Twain".

Friday, August 23.

Victoria. Mark and I were out all day getting books, cigars, and tobacco. He bought 3,000 manilla cheroots, thinking that with four pounds of Durham smoking tobacco he could make the 3,000 cheroots last three weeks. If perpetual smoking ever kills a man, I don't see how "Mark Twain" can expect to escape. He and Mrs. Clemens, and an old friend, and his wife, now living near here[,] went for a drive and were out most of the day. This is remarkable for him. I never knew him to do such a thing before.

The "Warrimoo" arrived about one o'clock, and we all went on board and lunched together for the last time. Mrs. Clemens is disappointed in the ship. The whole thing looks discouraging, and our hearts are almost broken for the poor woman. She tells me she is going to brave it through, for she must do it. It is for her children. Our party got out on the deck of the "Warrimoo" and Mr. W. G. Chase, a passenger [,] took a snap shot of our quintette. Then wife and I went ashore, and the old ship started across the Pacific Ocean with three of our most beloved friends on board. We waved to one another as long as they kept in sight.

Just before sailing for Australia, in August, 1895, Mark Twain gave to the public, through the San Francisco Examiner, a remarkable statement regarding the firm debts which he had determined to pay, the success that had attended the American segment of this great tour under my management, and the effect upon himself, physically and mentally, of his lecturing experiences. As to the debts, he said:

"I furnished the capital for that concern. It made a fortune the first year, and wasted it in the second. After that it began to accumulate debts, and kept this industry diligently up until the collapse came. My wife and I tried our best to save it; we emptied money down that bottomless hole as long as we had a penny left, but the effort went for nothing. When the crash came the firm owed my wife almost as much as it owed all the other creditors put together. By the advice of friends I turned over to her my copyrights, she releasing the firm and taking this perishable property in full settlement of her claim—property not worth more than half the sum owing to her. She wanted to turn her house in, too, and leave herself and the children shelterless; but she hadn't a friend who would listen to that for a moment."

The money Mark earned in 1894, added to the assets, enabled him to pay off one-half of the great indebtedness. He wrote that,

"A month ago I supposed it would take me a dreary long time to earn the other half, but my eyes have been opened by this lecture trip across the continent. I find I have twenty-five friends in America where I thought I had only one…. Did those unknown friends troop to my houses in this perditionary weather to hear me talk? No; they came to shake hands and let me know that they were on deck and all was well. I shall be out of debt a long way sooner than I was supposing a month ago, before Cleveland spoke up and set the pace of my jog around the globe.

"I shall be 60 years old in November. A month ago it grieved me to be under this load of debt at my time of life, but that feeling is all gone now. Such a burden is a benefaction, a prize in the lottery of life, when it lifts a curtain and shows you a continual spread of personal friends where you had supposed you had merely a good sprinkling of folks friendly to your books, but not particularly concerned about their author.

• • • • •

"And so, let me sound my horn. It doesn't do you any harm, and I like the music of it.

"Properly, one-third of our dead firm's debts should be paid by my partner; but he has no resources. This is why I must pay them all. If I have time and health, I can do it, and I think the creditors have confidence in me. And my wife and children are not troubled. They never knew anything about scrimping before, but they have learned it now; they know all about it these last two years, and whatever murmuring is done I do—not they.

• • • • •

"My trip means a year's lecturing all around the world, and thereafter a lecture trip all over the United States, beginning either at New York or San Francisco—the latter, I expect. My agent was a little afraid of San Francisco in summer. He thought we couldn't fairly expect to get great audiences. Maybe he was right, but I doubted it. It has been one of my homes.

"Now that I reflect, perhaps it is a little immodest in me to talk about my paying my debts, when by my own confession I am blandly getting ready to unload them on to the whole English speaking world. I didn't think of that. Well, no matter, so long as they get paid.

"Lecturing is gymnastics, chest-expander, medicine, mind-healer, blues-destroyer, all in one. I am twice as well as I was when I started out; I have gained nine pounds in twenty-eight days, and expect to weigh 600 before January. I haven't had a blue day in all the twenty-eight. My wife and daughter are accumulating health and strength and flesh nearly as fast as I am. When we reach home a year hence I think we can exhibit as freaks.

Mark Twain
Vaancouver, B. C., Aug. 15, 1985."

On our return from seeing Mr. & Mrs. Clemens and their daughter Clara embark at Victoria, B.C., on the S. S. Warrimoo, for Australia and around the world, my wife and I paid a visit to "Quarry Farm" which has been the summer home of Mark Twain and his family for many years.

Quarry Farm, on the hill north of and overlooking Elmira, New York is owned by Mrs. S. L. Crane, a sister of Mrs. Clemens, with whom Susy and Gene, the eldest and youngest daughters, were left when Mr and Mrs C and Clara started in July 95 on the great tour around the world. There the Clemens children have spent their summers, playing about the beautiful grounds, from babyhood to womanhood. Mrs. Crane has no children of her own, but has hardly ever been able to realize that the young nieces were not as much to her as to their own mother.

It was my custom to visit Mark, when I had business with him, at this summer retreat, and it was here, in a beautiful rustic, outdoor study, which Mrs. Crane had built especially for the purpose, that "The Gilded Age," "The Prince and the Pauper," "Tom Sawyer," and other of the great humorist's books were written.

Mark's favorite domestic animal is the cat, and on Quarry Farm he was invariably accompanied by a drove of cats. They followed him wherever he strolled about the place. By his desk in his bower study and by his side at the table was a large chair which they occupied if he were there. He had for a long time a quartette of the handsomest specimens I ever saw, and they were under complete control. He would call them to "come up" on the chair, and simultaneously they all jumped on the seat. He would tell them, "Go to sleep," and instantly the group were all apparently fast asleep and would remain that way until he called, "Wide awake," when up went their ears and wide open their eyes. The accompanying pictures Mark had taken of his four especial favorites, whose names were Beelzebub, Blatherskite, Apollonius and Buffalo Bill. The pictures were presented to me by Mrs. Crane.

On September 17th, 1897, he wrote to me from Weggis, Lake Lucerne: —

"I feel quite sure that in Cape Town, 13 months ago, I stood on a platform for the last time. Nothing but the Webster debts could persuade me to lecture again, and I have ceased to worry about those. You remember in the Sam Moffett interview in Vancouver, in '95, I gave myself four years in which to make money enough to pay those debts—and that included two lecture seasons in America, one in England, and one around the world. But the Madam and I are well satisfied now that we shall have those debts paid off a year earlier than the prophecy, if I continue able to work as I have been working in London and here, *and without any further help from the platform*. And so it is as I said a moment ago, I am a cheerful man these days.

"It is the madam's economical genius that is accomplishing this. She knows where every penny goes, and that it does not go unnecessarily. She was reared in wealth, and therefore she knows the actual—not the imaginary—value of money".
In another letter he said:

"I managed to pull through that long lecture campaign, but I was never very well, from the first night in Cleveland to the last one in Cape Town, and I found it pretty hard work on that account. I did a good deal of talking when I ought to have been in bed. At present I am not strong enough for platform work, and am not going to allow myself to think of London, or any other platform, for a long time to come. It grieves me, for I could make a satisfactory season in London and America, now that I am practiced in my trade again."
On April 4th, 1899, he wrote me from Vienna: —

"No,--- I don't like lecturing. I lectured in Vienna two or three weeks ago, and in Budapest last week, but it was merely for fun, not for money. I charged nothing in Vienna, and only the family's expenses in Budapest. I like to talk for nothing, about twice a year, but talking for money is *work*, and that takes the pleasure out of it. I do not believe you could offer me terms that would dissolve my prejudice against the platform. I do not expect to see a platform again until the wolf commands.--- Honest people do not go robbing the public on the platform, except when they are in debt. (Disseminate this idea---it can do good)".

In the autumn of '95, I wanted him to give fifty lectures in England, but he thought it would not be worth his while. His book was the next thing to be thought of and planned for. <One year> Four years later while he was in Sweden, I again suggested lecturing at a thousand dollars a night. "I think there's stuff in 'Following the Equator' for a lecture, but I can't come", he wrote.

As a letter-writer, Mark Twain is inimitable. He writes with the same unconventionality with which he talks, and his letters are the man.

"Dear Pond,
O, b'gosh, I can't. I hate writing.
Ever thine,
Mark",
is characteristic. "Hold on!" "Oh, come now!" "Oh, dang it, I'm head over heels in hard work on a book", "sho---go 'long!" "Lead us not into temptation, b'gosh!" "Goway! you and his reverence. Tempt me not", are such

expressions as give personality to his letters.

In the autumn of 1899 he wrote to me, "I'm not going to barnstorm the platform any more, but I am glad you have corraled Howells. He's a most sinful man and I always knew God would send him to the platform, if he didn't behave".

In another letter, "Say! some time ago I received notice that I had been elected as honorary member of the 'Society of Sons of Steerage Immigrants', and was told that Kipling, Hop Smith and Nelson Page are officers of it. What right have they to belong ? Ask Page or Smith about it".

"Mark Twain" eats only when he is hungry. I have known him to go days without eating a particle of food: at the same time he would be smoking constantly when he was not sleeping. He insisted that the stomach would call when in need, and it did. I have known him to sit for hours in a smoking car on a cold day, smoking his pipe and reading his Dutch book, with the window wide open. I said once, "Mark, do you know it's a cold day and you are exposing yourself before that open window, and you are booked to lecture to-night?"

"I do — know — all — about it. I am letting some of God's fresh air into my lungs for that purpose. My stomach is all right and under these conditions I am not afraid of taking cold".

"But", said I, "the car is cold and you are making the passengers uncomfortable by insisting on that window being wide open".

"They deserve to be uncomfortable for not knowing how to live and take care of themselves". He closed the window however. Mark never had a cold, and with the exception of carbuncles was never ill.

Mark's appreciation of Frank Mayo was very sincere. "Pudd'nhead Wilson" was first acted by Mayo[.] <After> Seeing it for the first time at the Herald Square theatre, the audience discovered him in a box and Mark was vociferously call[ed] "Mark Twain! Mark Twain!!" He rose right up and said:

> "I am sure I could say many complimentary things about this
> play which Mr. Mayo has written, and about his portrayal of
> the chief character in it, and keep well within the bounds both
> of fact and of good taste; but I will limit myself to two or three.
> I do not know how to utter any higher praise than this; that
> when Mayo's Pudd'nhead walks this stage here, clothed in the

charm of his gentle charities of speech, and acts the sweet simplicities and sincerities of his gracious nature, the thought in my mind is, Why, bless your heart, you couldn't be any dearer or lov[e]lier or sweeter than you are without turning into that man whom all men love, and even Satan is fond of—Joe Jefferson."

Continuation of Mark Twain's speech at the theatre when "Pudd'nhead Wilson" was first produced.

"I am gratified to see that Mr. Mayo has been able to manage those difficult twins. I tried, but in my hands they failed. When I was here year before last, there was an Italian freak on exhibition in Philadelphia who was an exaggeration of the Siamese twins. This freak had one body, one pair of legs, two heads and four arms. I thought he would be useful in a book, so I put him in. And then the trouble began. I called these consolidated twins Angelo and Luigi, and I tried to make them nice and agreeable, but it was not possible. They would not do anything my way, but only their own. They were wholly unmanageable, and not a day went by that they didn't develop some new kind of devilishness—particularly Luigi. Angelo was of a religious turn of mind and was monotonously honest and honorable and upright, and tediously proper; whereas Luigi had no principles, no morals, no religion—a perfect blatherskite, and an inextricable tangle, theologically—infidel, atheist and agnostic all mixed together. He was of a malicious disposition, and liked to eat things which disagreed with his brother. They were so strangely organized that what one of them ate or drank had no effect upon himself, but only nourished or damaged the other one. Luigi was hearty and robust because Angelo ate the best and most wholesome food he could find for him; but Angelo was himself delicate and sickly because every day Luigi filled him up with mince pies and salt junk just because he knew he couldn't digest them. Luigi was very dissipated, but it didn't show on him, but only on his brother. His brother was a strict and conscientious teetoler, but he was drunk most of the time, on account of Luigi's habits. Angelo was President of the Prohibition Society, but they had to turn him out, because every time he appeared at the head of the procession on parade he was a scandalous spectacle to look at. On the other hand Angelo was a trouble to Luigi the infidel, because he was always changing his religion, trying to find the best one, and he always preferred sects that believed in baptism by immersion, and this was a constant peril and discomfort to Luigi, who couldn't stand water outside or in; so every time Angleo got baptised Luigi got drowned, and had to be pumped out and resuscitated. Luigi was irascible, yet was never willing to stand by the consequences of his acts. He was always kicking somebody and then laying it on Angelo. And when the kicked person kicked back, Luigi would say, "What are you kicking me for? I haven't done anything to you." Then the man would be sorry, and say, "Well, I didn't mean any harm, I thought it was you; but you see, you people have only one body between you, and I can't tell which of you I'm kicking. I don't know how to discriminate. I do not wish to be unfair, and so there is no way for me to do but to kick one of you and apologize to the other." They were a troublesome pair in every way. If they did any work for you, they charged for two; but at the boarding house they ate and slept for two and paid for only one. It was the same at the theatre. Luigi bought one ticket and deadheaded Angelo in. They couldn't put Angelo out because they couldn't put the deadhead out without putting out the twin that had paid, and scooping in a suit for damages.

"Luigi grew steadily more and more wicked, and I saw by and by from the way he was going on that he was bound to land in the eternal tropics, and at bottom I was glad of it; but I knew he would necessarily take his righteous brother down there with him, and that would not be fair. I did not object to it, but I didn't want to be responsible for it. I was in such a hobble that there was only one way out. To save the righteous brother I had to pull the consolidated twins apart and make two separate and distinct twins of them. Well, as soon as I did that, they lost all their energy and took no further interest in life. They were wholly futile and useless in the book; they became mere shadows, and so they remain. Mr. Mayo manages them, but if he had taken a chance at them before I pulled them apart and tamed them he would have found out early that if he put them in his play they would take full possession and there wouldn't be any room in it for Pudd'nhead Wilson or anybody else.

"I have taken four days to prepare these statistics, and as far as they go you can depend upon their being strictly true. I have not told all the truth about the twins, but just barely enough of it for business purposes, for my motto is—and Pudd'nhead Wilson can adopt it if he wants to—my motto is, 'Truth is the most valuable thing we have; let us economize it.'"

In May, 1895, he wrote to me from Paris, "Frank Mayo has done a great thing for both of us; for he has proved himself a gifted dramatist as well as a gifted orator, and has enabled me to add another new character to American drama. I hope he will have grand success."

The serious side of Mark Twain is shown in the following letter to a woman whose sister wished to go upon the lecture platform. The letter also points a moral.

"I have seen it tried many and many a time. I have seen a lady lecturer urged upon the public in a lavishly complimentary document signed by Longfellow, Whittier, Holmes, and some others of supreme celebrity, but—there was nothing in her and she failed. If there had been any great merit in her she never would have needed those men's help; and (at her rather mature age) would never have consented to ask it.

["]There is an unwritten law about human successes, and your sister must bow to that law. She must submit to its requirements. In brief, this law is:—

1. No occupation without an apprenticeship.

2. No pay to the apprentice.

["]This law stands right in the way of the subaltern who wants to be a general before he has smelt powder; and it stands (and should stand) in everybody's way who applies for pay and position before he has served his apprenticeship and proved himself. Your sister's course is perfectly plain. Let her enclose this letter to Major J. B. Pond, Everet House[,] New York[,] and offer to lecture a year for $10.00 a week and her expenses, the contract to be annullable by him at any time after a month's notice, but not annullable by her at all. The second year, he to have her services, if he wants them, at a trifle under the best price offered by anybody else.

["]She can learn her trade in those two years, and then be entitled to remuneration—but she cannot learn it in any less time than that, unless she is a human miracle.

["]Try it, and do not be afraid. It is the fair and right thing. If she wins, she will win squarely and righteously, and never have to blush."

No man has ever written whose humor has so many sides, or such breadth and reach. His passages provoke the joyous laughter of young and old, of learned and unlearned, and may be read the hundredth time without losing but rather multiplying in power. Sentences and phrases that seem at first made only for the heartiest laughter, yield at closer view a sanity and wisdom that is good for the soul. He is also a wonderful storyteller. Thousands of people can bear testimony that the very humor which has made him known all over the world is oftentimes swept along like the debris of a freshet by the current of his fascinating narrative.

Business relations and travelling bring out the nature of a man. After my close relations with Mark Twain for sixteen years, I can say that he is not only what the world knows him to be, a humorist, a philosopher, and a genius, but a sympathetic, honest, brave gentleman.

James B. Pond's Photographs

Olivia Clemens, Samuel L. Clemens and Mrs. Pond enroute to the S. S. **Northland**. *Cleveland. July 17.*

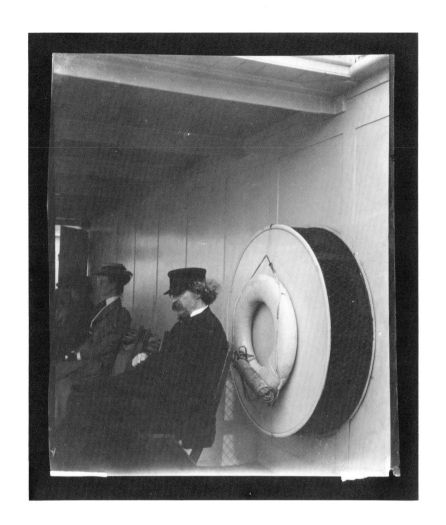

Upper left:
Mrs. Pond and Clemens aboard the S. S. **Northland**. Cleveland. July 17.

Upper right:
Clemens, Clara Clemens and Olivia aboard the S. S. **Northland**.
Leaving Cleveland. July 18.

Upper left:
*Olivia urging Clemens to wear his overcoat. Aboard the S. S. **Northland**. July 18.*

Upper right:
*Olivia urging Clemens to wear his overcoat. Aboard the S. S. **Northland**. July 18.*

Upper left:
Clemens aboard the S. S. **Northland**. July 18.

Upper right:
Mrs. Pond (foreground) and Olivia (at left) aboard the S. S. **Northland**. July 18.

26

Upper left:
Mrs. Pond aboard the T. S. **Faxton**. *July 19.*

Upper right:
Officer and guest aboard the T. S. **Faxton**. *July 19.*

Upper left:
Mackinaw Island from the T. S. **Faxton**. July 19.

Upper right:
Arrival at Mackinaw Island. From the T. S. **Faxton**. The Grand Hotel is in the distance.
July 19.

Clara and Clemens. Location uncertain. Probably
July 24th or 25th.

Olivia (at left) and Mrs. Pond aboard the train. July.

Upper left:
View from the train. July.

Lower left:
Unidentified individuals, Mrs. Pond, Clara. Roof of the Hotel Manitoba. July 26.

Upper right:
Clara and Mrs. Pond aboard the train. July.

Clara. Train Station. Gretna, Manitoba. July 26.

Upper left:
Olivia and Clemens. Gretna, Manitoba. July 26.

Upper right:
The party waiting to pass customs. Gretna, Manitoba. July 26.

Upper left:
Major Pond (center) and Clara.(Clemens and Olivia visible over Clara's shoulder.)
Gretna, Manitoba. July 26.

Upper right:
Clemens (seated) and Olivia, Mrs. Pond and Clara (foreground). Gretna, Manitoba.
July 26.

Upper left:
View of Winnipeg from the roof of the Hotel Manitoba. July 26.

Lower left:
View of Winnipeg from the roof of the Hotel Manitoba. July 26.

Upper right:
Clemens. Gretna, Manitoba. July 26.

Clara, Mrs. Pond, Major Pond. Roof of the Hotel Manitoba. Winnipeg, Manitoba. July 26.

Upper left:
Clara with English host (foreground), Mrs. Pond and Olivia. Winnipeg, Manitoba.
July 27.

Lower left:
Clara, Mrs. Pond and Olivia with young English gentlemen. Winnipeg, Manitoba.
July 27.

Upper right:
Olivia and English gentleman (in carriage at left), Clara and Mrs. Pond with English
gentlemen (in carriage at right). Buffalo enclosure. Winnipeg, Manitoba. July 27.

Upper left:
Olivia and English gentleman (in carriage at left), Clara and Mrs. Pond with English gentlemen (in carriage at right). Buffalo enclosure. Winnipeg, Manitoba. July 27.

Upper right:
Buffalo enclosure. Winnipeg, Manitoba. July 27.

Lower right:
Clara and English gentleman. Buffalo enclosure. Winnipeg, Manitoba. July 27.

Clara, Mrs. Pond and Olivia with Englishmen. Winnipeg, Manitoba. July 27.

Clemens, Mrs. Pond and Major Pond. Winnipeg, Manitoba.

The party and other travelers departing Winnipeg.

Mrs. Pond, Major Pond, Clemens and Olivia. Waiting for the train. Five A.M. Crookston, Minnesota. July 30.

Clemens, Mrs. Pond, Olivia and Clara.
Grand Fork, North Dakota. July 30.

Upper left:
Leaving Grand Fork, North Dakota. July 30.

Upper right:
Clemens. Railroad station. Great Falls, Montana. July 31.

Upper left:
Clemens. Railroad station. Great Falls, Montana. July 31.

Upper right:
Great Falls, Montana. July 31.

Lower right:
Mrs. Pond. Great Falls, Montana. July 31.

Upper left:
Mrs. Pond and Major Pond. Great Falls, Montana. July 31.

Upper right:
Mrs. Pond and Clara. Great Falls, Montana. July 31.

Lower right:
Clara, Clemens, Mrs. Pond, Gibson and Olivia. Great Falls, Montana. July 31.

Mrs. Pond and Clara. Great Falls, Montana. July 31.

Upper left:
"Giant Springs." Great Falls, Montana. July 31.

Upper right:
Clara. "Giant Springs." Great Falls, Montana. July 31.

Lower right:
Major and Mrs. Pond. Great Falls, Montana. July 31.

48

Gibson, Clara, Olivia, Clemens and Mrs. Pond. "Giant Springs." Great Falls, Montana. July 31.

49

Upper left:
Clemens. Norwegian Shanty Town. Great Falls, Montana. July 31.

Upper right:
Norwegian Shanty Town. Great Falls, Montana. July 31.

Lower right:
Norwegian Shanty Town. Great Falls, Montana. July 31.

Clemens. Norwegian Shanty Town. Great Falls, Montana. July 31.

Upper left:
Clemens and little girl. Norwegian Shanty Town. Great Falls, Montana. July 31.

Upper right:
The little girl hesitates. Norwegian Shanty Town. Great Falls, Montana. July 31.

Clemens with kittens and the little girl's family. Norwegian Shanty Town. Great Falls, Montana. July 31.

Upper left:
Clemens and the little girl's family. Norwegian Shanty Town. Great Falls, Montana.
July 31.

Upper right:
Clemens leaving the little girl and her family. Norwegian Shanty Town.
Great Falls, Montana. July 31.

*Clemens and D. C. K. Cole. Lobby of the Helena
Hotel. Helena, Montana. August 4.*

Clemens and Senator Sanders. Missoula, Montana.
August 5.

Mrs. Henry Ward Beecher, Senator Sanders and Clemens. Missoula, Montana. August 5.

57

Upper left:
Mrs. Henry Ward Beecher and Senator Sanders. Missoula, Montana. August 5.

Upper right:
Mrs. Henry Ward Beecher and unidentified individuals. Missoula, Montana. August 5.

Upper left:
Major Pond, Clara, Clemens and Olivia. Probably Missoula, Montana.

Lower left:
Man on a bicycle leading a horse to the blacksmiths shop. "The decadence of the horse."
Missoula, Montana. August 5.

Upper right:
Clemens and soldiers. Fort Missoula, Montana. August 6.

Clemens and Officers. Fort Missoula, Montana.
August 6.

Upper left:
Clemens and Colonel Burt. Fort Missoula, Montana. August 6.

Lower left:
Mrs. Pond, Clara, Olivia, Clemens and Colonel Burt. Fort Missoula, Montana.
August 6.

Upper right:
Montana (undated). (Possibly August 2?)

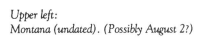

Upper left:
Montana (*undated*). (*Possibly August 2?*)

Upper right:
Clara (*undated*).

Lower right:
Mrs. Pond, Olivia, Clara (*undated*).

Upper left:
Olivia, Major Pond, Mrs. Pond (undated).

Upper right:
I. O. O. F. Hall. Location unknown.

Clemens and Clara (Location unknown).

Clemens. (Location unknown)

Upper left:
Clemens aboard the engine. The Great Northern. August 8/9.

Upper right:
Major Pond aboard the engine. The Great Northern. August 8/9.

Mrs. Pond, Clara, Clemens and Major Pond. Crossing the Rockies. The Great Northern. August 9.

Clemens aboard the steamer **Flyer.** *Seattle. August 8.*

Upper left:
Mrs. Pond, Clara and Olivia. Tacoma Hotel. Tacoma, Washington.

Upper right:
Clemens and reporters. Columbia River Ferry. Portland, Oregon. August 9.

Upper left:
Clemens and reporters. Columbia River Ferry. Portland, Oregon. August 9.

Upper right:
Reporters, Clemens and Major Pond. Columbia River Ferry. Portland, Oregon.
August 9.

Lower right:
Reporter and Clemens. Columbia River Ferry. Portland, Oregon. August 9.

Mr. Pearce of the **Portland Oregonian** and
Clemens. Portland, Oregon. August 9.

Clemens in Hotel room. Olympia, Washington. August 11.

Upper left:
Clara, Mrs. Pond, Olivia and Samuel Moffett aboard the steamer **Flyer***. Tacoma,*
Washington. August 13.

Lower left:
Samuel Moffett, Olivia, Clara, Clemens, unidentified guest, Mrs. Pond and Officer
aboard the U. S. S. **Mohican***. August 13.*

Upper right:
Clara, Clemens, Samuel Moffett and Olivia aboard the steamer **Flyer***. Tacoma,*
Washington. August 13.

*Clemens aboard the U. S. S. **Mohican**.*
Seattle, Washington. August 13.

74

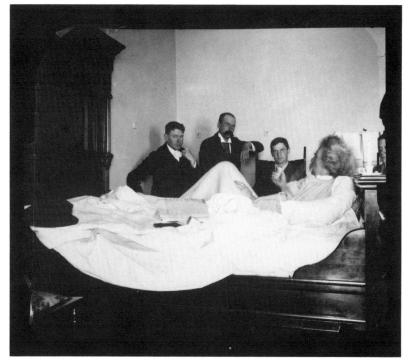

Upper left:
S. S. **Warimoo**. Victoria, British Columbia. August 23.

Upper right:
Clara, Olivia and Mrs. Pond. The S. S. **Warimoo**. Victoria, British Columbia.
August 23.

Lower right:
Major Pond, Clemens, Clara and Olivia aboard the S. S. **Warimoo**.
Victoria, British Columbia. August 23.

Clemens, Clara, and Olivia aboard the S. S. **Warimoo**. *Victoria, British Columbia. August 23.*

Upper left:
Clemens aboard the S. S. **Warimoo**. *Victoria, British Columbia. August 23.*

Upper right:
S. S. **Warimoo** *sailing for Australia. August 23.*

Quarry Farm and Elmira   *Unidentified individual, Susy Clemens, Bim Pond, Susan Crane, Major Pond and Mrs. Pond. Quarry Farm. Elmira, New York. September 15.*

79

Susan Crane, Mrs. Pond, Bim, Susy, and the dogs, Osmon and Bruce. Quarry Farm. Elmira, New York. September 15.

Upper left:
Susan Crane, Mrs. C. J. Langdon, Major Pond, Bim, Susy, C. J. Langdon and Mrs. Pond. Quarry Farm. Elmira, New York. September 15.

Lower left:
Bim, Susan Crane, Osmon and Susy. Quarry Farm. Elmira, New York. September 15.

Upper right:
Unidentified individual, Jean Clemens, unidentified individual, Bim, unidentified individual, Bruce, Osmon and Susan Crane. Quarry Farm. Elmira, New York. September 15.

Mrs. Pond, C. J. Langdon, unidentified individual, Susan Crane and unidentified individual. Quarry Farm. Elmira, New York. September 15.

Susan Crane, Bim, Susy and Mrs. Pond. **Quarry** *Farm. Elmira, New York. September 15.*

Susan Crane, Bim and Osmon. Quarry Farm. Elmira, New York. September 15.

Jean (on the roof), Bim, Osmon, Bruce and Susan Crane. September 15.

Upper left:
Bim, Susan Crane and Osmon. Quarry Farm. Elmira, New York. September 15.

Upper right:
Bim. Quarry Farm. Elmira, New York. September 15.

Lower right:
Osmon, unidentified individual. Quarry Farm. Elmira, New York. September 15.

Upper left:
Bim. Quarry Farm. Elmira, New York. September 15.

Lower left:
Susan Crane, Osmon, Bim and Mrs. Pond. Quarry Farm. Elmira, New York.
September 15.

Upper right:
The view from Quarry Farm. Elmira, New York. September 15.

Mrs. Pond, Bim, Susan Crane and Osmon. Quarry Farm. Elmira, New York. September 15.

Upper left:
Bim, Susy, Osmon, Susan Crane and Mrs. Pond. The tent. Quarry Farm.
Elmira, New York. September 15.

Lower left:
Susan Crane, Bim and Mrs. Pond. The tent. Quarry Farm. Elmira, New York.
September 15.

Upper right:
Mrs. Pond, Julia Beecher and Bim. The Beecher home. East Hill. Elmira, New York.
September 16.

Upper left:
Bim. Quarry Farm. Elmira, New York. September 15.

Upper right:
Mrs. Pond.

Lower right:
Major Pond.

A Note About the Editors

Alan Gribben

Alan Gribben served as a research editor for the Mark Twain Papers in the Bancroft Library at the University of California at Berkeley before joining the faculty of the University of Texas at Austin in 1974. Ten years of his study of Twain's reading culminated in *Mark Twain's Library: A Reconstruction* (2 vols., 1980). Professor Gribben has also published numerous articles about Twain's literary reputation and works as well as an edition of Edith Wharton's letters. He was the co-founder and president of the Mark Twain Circle of America, a national scholarly society. In 1987 he became the first recipient of the Jervis Langdon, Jr. Research Fellowship-in-Residence bestowed by the Elmira College Center for Mark Twain Studies at Quarry Farm, and in 1990 he received its Certificate of Award for his "lasting contributions to Mark Twain studies." In 1991 he joined the faculty of Auburn University at Montgomery, Alabama, where he holds the rank of Professor and serves as head of the Department of English and Philosophy.

Nick Karanovich

Nick Karanovich is a graduate of Indiana University and has completed post-graduate work at St. Francis College, Ball State University, and Harvard University. He has lectured on Mark Twain around the country, and has given presentations for the Lilly Library at Indiana University, U.S. Naval Academy at Annapolis, Baltimore Bibliophiles at Johns Hopkins University, and the Elmira College Center for Mark Twain Studies at Quarry Farm. Mr. Karanovich has published *A Book Collecting Melange* (1983), "A Suppressed Mark Twain Chapter" in *The American Book Collector* (1984), *A Mark Twain Collector's List* (1985), and "Sixty Books From Mark Twain's Library" in *The Mark Twain Journal* (1987). He has also contributed entries for the forthcoming *Mark Twain Encyclopedia*. Items from his Mark Twain collection were featured in an exhibition at Indiana University's Lilly Rare Book Library in the spring of 1991; a catalogue of this exhibition included the first appearance in print of more than forty previously unpublished Mark Twain letters. His Mark Twain holdings have been described as "both the finest and most extensive in private hands."

The Center and Its Programs

Overland with Mark Twain is a publication of the Elmira College Center for Mark Twain Studies at Quarry Farm. The Center was established in 1983 following the gift of a 6.7 acre portion of Quarry Farm to Elmira College from Mark Twain's grandnephew, Jervis Langdon, Jr. Here, throughout the 1870s and 1880s, Mark Twain summered and wrote the major portions of his most important books.

In addition to its publications, the Center also sponsors a program of fellowships-in-residence, a distinguished academic visitors series, public talks and chamber theater, lesson visits for school groups, special presentations for community groups, summer seminars and institutes for teachers, and colloquia and conferences. Through its activities and programs, the Center seeks to foster and support significant Mark Twain studies, increase public understanding and appreciation of Mark Twain, and strengthen the teaching of Mark Twain at all academic levels.

Center facilities at Quarry Farm include a spacious Victorian home with a grand porch and commanding view of the Chemung River valley, two adjoined cottages, a large barn, and the original site of Mark Twain's famous octagonal study, which was removed to the College's campus in 1952. The main house is utilized as a private residence for research fellows-in-residence and other visiting scholars. The cottages and barn have been renovated for use as office, conference, and public assembly spaces.

Fellows-in-residence at the Center receive free lodging at Quarry Farm for a period of two weeks to two months and have access to the John S. Tuckey Memorial Library of more than two hundred and fifty volumes of Mark Twain studies shelved at Quarry Farm and to the Mark Twain Archives located at the nearby Elmira College campus. The Archives consist of substantial microfilm portions of the major Twain collections located at Berkeley, Hartford, and Vasssar; an extensive collection of Mark Twain first editions; an exhaustive assemblage of biography, criticism, and reference sources; many association volumes containing Twain's own marginalia; and an extensive collection of photographs.

Public access to Quarry Farm is restricted to scheduled program events to assure resident scholars the same privacy and quiet that Mark Twain enjoyed when he summered here.

Center publications make available varied contributions to Mark Twain studies. We are especially grateful to the Mark Twain Foundation of New York City and the Wurtele Foundation of Elmira, New York, for continuing support of Quarry Farm programs. For additional information about the Center and its programs, write to the Center for Mark Twain Studies at Quarry Farm, Elmira College, Elmira, New York 14901, or telephone (607) 732-0993.

Darryl Baskin
Director

Quarry Farm Volumes

Overland with Mark Twain: James B. Pond's Photographs and Journal of the North American Lecture Tour of 1895, ed. Alan Gribben and Nick Karanovich. 1992.

Quarry Farm Papers

No. 1. Henry Nash Smith, *How True Are Dreams?: The Theme of Fantasy in Mark Twain's Later Work,* with a Foreword by Alan Gribben. 1989.

No. 2. John S. Tuckey, *Mark Twain: The Youth Who Lived on in the Sage,* with a Foreword by Howard Baetzhold. 1990.

No. 3 Lorraine Welling Lanmon, *Quarry Farm: A Study of the "Picturesque."* 1991.